"It is a privilege for me to endorse *T/ ing*. It is co-authored by two very dea the faith. They are blazing a way forw: to see the miraculous stories of the N transform lives and ministry. This boo transform you. It will revolutionize your life and ministry."

John Arnott, Catch the Fire Ministries, Toronto

"*The Essential Guide to Healing* is an excellent teaching tool that points us not only to God's power but also to the very nature of Jesus. Healings and miracles reveal God's huge heart of love. Read this book and watch God do wonders through you."

Heidi Baker, founding director, Iris Global

"Randy Clark and Bill Johnson lay out a solid biblical foundation and offer the practical and profound wisdom of both men's powerful healing ministries. Randy lays out a helpful historical and theological background for healing and the gifts of the Spirit. Bill gives a persuasive, big-picture view of how God wants heaven to invade earth through us, the Body of Christ. I highly recommend this book."

Gary S. Greig, former associate professor of Old Testament and Hebrew, School of Divinity, Regent University

"God is working in ways that surprise many of us. We may well not all agree how to understand all the details, but the experiences in this book challenge us to learn more about God's power and about His loving care for the afflicted."

Craig Keener, professor of New Testament, Asbury Theological Seminary

"Randy Clark and Bill Johnson are the leading teachers of our time on the theology and practice of Christian healing. Their book *The Essential Guide to Healing* is a precious gift to all of us who want to see prayer-mediated healing integrated into the wider world of evidence-based medicine."

Martin Moore-Ede, M.D., Ph.D.; chairman, Global Medical Research Institute; former professor, Harvard Medical School

"Randy Clark and Bill Johnson have a passion for healing and have inspired and activated countless 'little old me's' around the world to pray for the sick and see them recover. Bill and Randy are honest about their struggles in pursuing healing. This encourages all of us to step out of the box and seek first the Kingdom of God, which includes healing."

David Zaritzky, M.D., High Point, North Carolina

"You will be riveted by *The Essential Guide to Healing*, by both the theology of healing so clearly explained and the practical applications. Some parts of healing remain a holy mystery in God, but it has been written that God reveals His secrets to His friends. Since Randy and Bill are known as friends of God, that may explain why there is so much wisdom and revelation packed into one volume."

Steve Mory, M.D., Nashville, Tennessee

"*The Essential Guide to Healing* is a precious jewel for God's healing. The truthful heart of Christ's love for the afflicted overflows through this guide. It is a must-read for all pastors and leaders of the church."

Andrew Sung Park, professor of theology and ethics, United Theological Seminary, Dayton, Ohio

"*The Essential Guide to Healing* honestly fulfills the promise of its title. These authors are both gifted mightily in healing and provide a profoundly biblical, historical and reasoned case for their experiences. *Essential Guide* is simply the most balanced, informed and useful book on healing I've seen."

Jon Mark Ruthven, professor emeritus of theology, School of Divinity, Regent University; author, *On the Cessation of the Charismata*

"Bill Johnson and Randy Clark have capably captured the essence of training believers to engage in healing ministry effectively and confidently. *The Essential Guide to Healing* will stir more people to step out with faith and passion to fulfill Jesus' Kingdom call to heal the sick."

Paul L. King, D.Min., D.Th.; professor, Oral Roberts University; author, *God's Healing Arsenal*

*The*
# ESSENTIAL
# GUIDE
*to*
# HEALING

### EQUIPPING ALL CHRISTIANS
### *to* PRAY *for the* SICK

## BILL JOHNSON
## RANDY CLARK

**Chosen**
*a division of Baker Publishing Group*
Minneapolis, Minnesota

© 2011 by Bill Johnson and Randy Clark

Published by Chosen Books
11400 Hampshire Avenue South
Bloomington, Minnesota 55438
www.chosenbooks.com

Chosen Books is a division of
Baker Publishing Group, Grand Rapids, Michigan

Printed in the United States of America

Library of Congress Cataloging-in-Publication Data
Johnson, Bill.
    The essential guide to healing: equipping all christians to pray for the sick /
Bill Johnson, Randy Clark.
        p.   cm.
    Includes bibliographical references.
    ISBN 978–0–8007–9519–1 (pbk. : alk. paper)
    1. Spiritual healing—Christianity. I. Clark, Randy, 1952– II. Title.
BT732.5.J59 2011
234'.131—dc23                                                         2011025241

Unless otherwise indicated, Scripture quotations in Bill's chapters are from the New American Standard Bible®, copyright © 1960, 1962, 1963, 1968, 1971, 1972, 1973, 1975, 1977, 1995 by The Lockman Foundation. Used by permission.

Unless otherwise indicated, Scripture quotations in Randy's chapters are taken from the HOLY BIBLE, NEW INTERNATIONAL VERSION®. Copyright © 1973, 1978, 1984 Biblica. Used by permission of Zondervan. All rights reserved.

Scripture quotations identified AMP are from the Amplified® Bible, copyright © 1954, 1958, 1962, 1964, 1965, 1987 by The Lockman Foundation. Used by permission.

Scripture quotations identified HCSB are from the Holman Christian Standard Bible, copyright 1999, 2000, 2002, 2003 by Holman Bible Publishers. Used by permission.

Scripture quotations identified NKJV are from the New King James Version. Copyright © 1982 by Thomas Nelson, Inc. Used by permission. All rights reserved.

Scripture quotations identified KJV are from the King James Version of the Bible.

The Internet addresses, email addresses and phone numbers in this book are accurate at the time of publication. They are provided as a resource. Baker Publishing Group does not endorse them or vouch for their content or permanence.

Cover design by Kirk DouPonce, DogEared Design

18   19   20   21   22   23      16   15   14   13   12   11

# DEDICATION
# AND
# ACKNOWLEDGMENTS

I dedicate this book to the staff and students of Bethel School of Supernatural Ministry. The price that they have paid to carry this culture, to carry this anointing to the nations of the world is beyond inspiring. Their willingness to follow Jesus at any cost has brought me great courage. Thanks.

I write with great indebtedness to John Wimber and Randy Clark. When I heard John Wimber speak in 1987, I realized that a supernatural lifestyle was possible even for a normal person. That gave me the courage to try to minister to the sick outside the context of a church service or crusade, so public places became the setting in which I learned about the miracle power of Jesus. But I never met John. All I learned was from a distance, until I met Randy Clark. Randy has been the largest contributor to my understanding and experience of the miracle lifestyle. Before he came to Redding, we saw miracles weekly. After a few days with Randy, we saw the miracles multiply until they became daily happenings. John and Randy deserve much honor for lovingly sharing their lives with the rest of us.

Finally, I would like to thank and honor James Goll for his prophetic ministry to the Church at large. He was the one who prophesied to me about co-authoring a book with my dear friend Randy Clark. This book is in response to that word.

Much thanks also to Mary Berck for helping me gather my materials and to Pam Spinosi for her editing skills.

Bill Johnson

I dedicate this book to my wonderful wife, DeAnne. I would not be able to do what I am doing without her allowing me to be away for over 225 days a year. She shares in all the fruit of my ministry, and her reward in heaven will be great.

I also dedicate this book to John Wimber and Blaine Cook, who taught me so many of the concepts and so much of the language that I use in the healing ministry today. I will be forever grateful to them for introducing me to words of knowledge for healing the sick. A good portion of the models that I use come from John Wimber, and I received an impartation from both John and Blaine.

I want to thank my best friend and partner in ministry, Bill Johnson. He has been a continual source of encouragement and has challenged me to press in for greater levels of healing.

Finally, I have been blessed with a dedicated and talented editor, Trish Konieczny. She has kept me on track throughout this project and has been a great asset to Bill and me. This book probably would have been six hundred pages without her editing. I also want to thank editorial director Jane Campbell at Chosen for her many efforts in working on an outline, making suggestions and editing the text. Without her, this project might never have happened. It has been a great pleasure to work with Jane, as well as with marketing director Tim Peterson and the rest of the Chosen team.

Randy Clark

# CONTENTS

# INTRODUCTION

## *Randy*

It is only fair that I let you know I am not writing from an impartial, neutral, dispassionate position. No, I am passionate about healing. I believe in healing. I have experienced physical healing personally, as well as emotional healing. And I have been used to bring healing to thousands of others.

Furthermore, I am not apologetic for being partial in my opinions on the subject of healing. This subject cannot be understood or experienced from the detached, unbiased position of a reporter. To properly understand healing, one must experience it. When it comes to healing, knowledge without experience is an inferior level of knowledge.

This book has dual authorship. I am Randy Clark, and my co-author is Bill Johnson. We come from quite different backgrounds and experiences, but our lives have been connected by the Holy Spirit. We love and honor each other, and we have greatly encouraged each other in the ministry of healing. We each have contributed chapters that connect together into the book you now hold.

The main purpose of this book is to encourage you to believe that God could use you to pray for the sick and work through you to heal them. These pages will also inspire you with people's stories about healing and educate you about not only how to pray for healing, but how to receive words of knowledge related to healing.

It is our hope that each of you will begin to pray for others to be healed after reading this book. It is our hope that some of you will discover that God has given you a gift of healing.

It is our belief that "more people get healed when more people pray for healing."

It is our promise to lay a biblical foundation within these pages for the practice of healing and for the belief that all Christians should be equipped to pray for the sick. We ask you to study the Scripture with us and do what the Bereans did in the book of Acts: "Now the Bereans were of more noble character than the Thessalonians, for they received the message with great eagerness and examined the Scriptures every day to see if what Paul said was true" (Acts 17:11).

Examine with us the biblical truths and the theological basis for believing that the practice of healing is part of the good news that the Kingdom of God is near. And because of this truth that the Kingdom of God is near, we must change the way we think about what is possible.

# Part 1

# OUR PERSONAL JOURNEYS IN REGARD TO HEALING

We tell our individual stories of how we grew in our faith for healing and were called into ministry. We also relate how we came to see that the gifts of the Holy Spirit in operation today are a demonstration of the Kingdom of God on the earth.

# 1

# RANDY'S JOURNEY

*Randy*

I regained consciousness to find myself looking out of a dark place, seeing light. I was inside an ambulance, looking out the back door that had not been closed yet. A high school friend was beside me.

I asked, "What happened?"

He responded, "You've been in a terrible accident."

I asked, "Is everyone okay?"

He responded, "It was a terrible accident. George is not badly hurt, but you have been, and so have Marge and Joe."

I was taken to our county hospital, where they X-rayed me and sewed up my forehead, eyebrow, cheekbone and under my jawbone. It took sixty stitches. My left eyebrow bone and cheekbone had been badly broken, my fractured jaw needed to be set and three places in my forehead hairline had been crushed. (Later I found out that doctors had debated about whether or not I should have a plate put in my head.

Thankfully, they did not do it.) I was in excruciating pain. It felt like someone had stabbed me in the back with a three-inch knife blade.

The doctors shortly transferred me by ambulance to a larger hospital in another county. During the ride, I slipped in and out of consciousness. My Grandmother Clark and my mother were in the ambulance with me. I remember coming to. My grandmother told me I was lucky to be alive. I responded by pointing my finger up toward heaven. I was in too much pain to talk. I remember thinking, *I'm sure glad I gave my life back to God four days ago. I have no fear of death because I know spiritually I'm ready to meet God. I* also remember thinking, *How different this would all be if I were still backslidden. To come so close to death and not be right with God would be a scary thing.*

The next few days were a blur. I drifted in and out of consciousness. Doctors inserted a tube through my nose to pump my stomach because my intestinal tract was paralyzed. They put in a catheter because my kidneys were not working properly. For days there was blood in my urine. I was sedated almost round the clock due to the intensity of the pain. I received 50 milligrams of Demerol every three hours, yet I would wake up from the effects of the medicine and ask for another shot to deaden the pain. My face was badly swollen, and my eyes were swollen shut for several days.

During this time, the doctors told my parents I would need hospitalization for seven to eleven weeks. In addition to my other injuries, I had a broken rib and thoracic disc and vertebrae damage. The impact of the accident had caused a 10–15 percent compression in my spine. Three specialists were treating me: an internist, an orthopedist and a neurologist. (In 2008 I would undergo an MRI for a different spinal problem. The doctor at that time asked me what I had done to my spine because the MRI revealed old fractures of almost every vertebrae. I told him it was from a car wreck thirty-eight years prior.)

I was told not to move because for several days after a spinal injury, the swelling can cause permanent damage. I could become paraplegic or suffer charley horse–like cramps for the rest of my life. If I needed to move, three nurses would logroll me, one at my shoulders, one at my waist and one near my knees. I could not even use a pillow.

In spite of all my injuries, I was optimistic. I told people I would be out of the hospital in time for an evangelistic crusade in four weeks at my home church, the First General Baptist Church in McLeansboro, Illinois. I actually was unaware of some of my injuries at the time.

Several days went by before I was finally told that my second-best friend, Joe Barker, had died from a broken neck in the accident. When my parents told me about Joe's death, they also showed me pictures of the car we were in. Hit by another car that had just come out of a banked S curve, it had flipped end over end, hit a telephone pole and landed upside down in a ditch. When I saw what the car looked like after all that, I thought, *It's a miracle that I lived! God spared my life—He must have a purpose for it.* I remember praying, "God, You spared my life. I give it back to You. I will do whatever You want with the rest of my life."

Not knowing how serious my injuries were, I was certain I would be out of the hospital in time to attend the upcoming evangelistic meetings, called a revival in Baptist churches. And God healed me—I left the hospital in twenty days.

How was I healed? In stages. First God healed the paralysis of my digestive system. I was scheduled for transfer to the largest hospital in St. Louis because of the paralysis.

But the night before the transfer, my friends at the church prayed for me at midnight. They felt a great peace and sensed I would be okay. When doctors examined me the next morning, my digestive system was working and the tube was removed.

Next, one of my specialists came to set my jaw. He said, "Put your teeth together. Do it again—again—*again*!" Then he said, "I don't understand! The X ray indicated that your jaw needed setting, but it's already set."

These words made me realize that God was indeed healing me. Two of my three major problems were healed already, though I was still in excruciating pain and still taking 50 milligrams of Demerol every three hours. Ministers visited to pray for my healing. My great-uncle, a Pentecostal preacher, came to pray. My pastor and his wife visited me to pray. After one extremely painful night, I woke up to discover that I felt no more pain. I remember thinking that morning, *God healed my jaw by setting it, and now I believe He has healed me of the severe pain!*

Then another thought came: *Get up and walk.*

I thought to myself, *The doctors emphasized that I am not to move my back. I am not to lift my head off the bed. I haven't even been allowed to use a pillow. I've been told that if I move, I could become paraplegic or have charley horses in my legs for life . . .*

Then the thought came again: *God has healed me. I should trust Him and try to walk.*

I believed God was encouraging me to get up and walk. I believed it so much that I slowly rose up in bed, let down the guardrail, slipped my feet over the side and then stepped out onto the floor. I grabbed the back of my air-conditioned hospital gown and held the two sides together, and I began to walk.

I walked out into the hallway. That was not smart! The nurses were very upset. They yelled at me and made me go back to bed. But I kept getting out of bed. I believed God had healed me. Finally, the head sister of St. Joseph Catholic Hospital came to talk with me. She told me how foolish I was being to risk permanent paralysis.

I told her, "I will not be paralyzed. God has healed me and has a purpose for my life."

She continued to appeal to my common sense. We went back and forth for a while, and finally I asked her, "You believe in God, don't you?"

"Yes, of course," she responded.

"So do I," I said, "and I believe in healing. God has healed me."

The doctor released me on the twentieth day and told me to go home and go to bed.

I told him, "I'm not going to bed. God has healed me, and I'm going to my church to testify about what God has done."

That night, a Wednesday, I went to church and shared with my youth group what God had done. I was eighteen. The following Sunday evening, the combined impact of my healing and Joe's death were instrumental in causing a true revival to break out in my church. It came a week ahead of the evangelistic meetings. The presence of God was so strong that the pastor called the evangelist and asked if he could come the very next night to continue what seemed like a revival outbreak among the high school youth.

The evangelist came, and our meetings lasted forty-two straight nights. It was in the middle of the Jesus Movement, and hundreds of high school youth attended from four surrounding counties. A high percentage of the students in my high school also came to this little Baptist church in true revival. Eleven young men from sixteen to twenty-three years old were called into the ministry during these meetings. I was one of them—but I am getting ahead of myself. I want to go further back in time and talk about a few other events that built my faith for healing.

## Why I Came to Believe in Healing

Three things happened that raised my interest in healing, and one thing caused me some doubt. First, when I was four or five, my maternal grandmother told me a story about her healing. I loved and respected my grandmother and thought of her as very spiritual. She was always singing hymns as she worked, and she loved to go to church, where she was a "shouter." She would sit on the left of the pulpit with other women "shouters," and I would sit with my grandpa on the right, in the "Amen corner" with other men. I found out later in life that the reason she always listened to Christian radio was that she was illiterate.

Grandma told me that one time in the bedroom of her little four-room, cement block house, she heard the audible voice of God tell her to go into the other bedroom and pray, then He would heal her. She had a large goiter in her throat at a time before doctors discovered how to treat them with iodine. She changed rooms, began to pray in obedience and felt something like a hot hand go down her throat. Her goiter disappeared. This healing made a huge impression on my little heart and mind.

The second thing that caused me to believe strongly in Jesus, heaven and the supernatural took place when I was six. It borders a little on the "out there" kind of experience some readers may find unnerving, but I believe my mother genuinely had a powerful experience with God through it. She had attended a home meeting where there had been worship and sharing. The meeting had not been overly emotional, and she left calmly to return home. On the way to the car, all of a sudden she felt as though she were caught in a whirlwind. She passed out and felt her spirit leaving her body. It went through a rough place followed by peace several times, and then she was in heaven. Jesus came and indicated to her that everything in her life was going to be okay. The experience repeated itself until she was back in her body. Then she came to.

I heard my mother tell this story many times. I did not think it was a psychological occurrence, but a very true, real experience. For over forty years Mom could not talk about it without losing it emotionally, overwhelmed with just the thought of her visit to heaven. When I was in college, I wrote a paper about Mom's experience. I interviewed the two men who had found her on the sidewalk while she was out of her body. They were both ministers by the time I interviewed them, though at the time of the incident they were not. They both told me that they could not find a pulse and that my mom was cold and clammy. They thought she had died.

Mom's experience, unusual though it may seem to some, made heaven more real to me. Jesus had talked to my mom in heaven! This was evidence to me that He had been raised from the dead, that He was still alive and that He still healed people.

The third thing that increased my faith in healing was the experience of my Sunday school teacher. She had been diagnosed with a tumor the size of a watermelon in her abdomen. Our church prayed for her the night before her surgery. When the surgery took place, the tumor had already shrunk to the size of an orange. Further, its roots were not attached to any organ and it was easily removed. This happened when I was about thirteen, and she lived another forty-plus years.

At sixteen, something happened that set back my faith in healing for a time. My maternal grandfather died of cancer at sixty-two. I had sat in the "Amen corner" with him at church, and I could not understand why he had not been healed. The same church that had prayed for my Sunday school teacher had prayed for him. Many churches were praying for him, yet he died. This caused me some doubt. I had just become a Christian the Sunday before my sixteenth birthday, and I lost Grandpa to cancer that same year. That was hard, and it was already a hard time for me. Along with some personal issues I struggled with, we were approaching the height of the Vietnam War. My high school's former heroes were coming home without legs. A young man who had been one year ahead of me in grade school came home in a body bag. It was a bad time to be approaching manhood. Angry over the war and depressed about a personal relationship gone wrong, I got involved with smoking marijuana on an almost daily basis for ten months. I wanted to experiment and started slipping into the drug culture, music and all. I wanted to visit the far country—but only visit it. I never wanted to stay there, so I stayed in church, too, though I knew I was a big hypocrite. Yet I was afraid to stop going to church, lest I become so deeply trapped in sin that I could not escape my self-made pigsty to return home.

A girlfriend's older brother was a Methodist preacher. He was the first person I ever saw hold a healing meeting in a church, and I liked and respected him. God used him to bring me under conviction. After not seeing me for a while, he commented to my mother that I did not seem like the Randy he remembered. I thought about that comment a lot. Four days before the accident that happened when I was eighteen, I got over my doubts and gave my heart back to God.

## A Call into Ministry

I mentioned briefly that I was called into ministry at eighteen, during the revival that followed my car accident. I want to share a little more about that. A healing was the culminating factor in my announcing my call to become a preacher. I had asked God to give me some signs confirming my call to preach, and immediately He answered two "fleeces" I placed before Him. The third sign He gave me was the healing.

My youth pastor, Fred, who was also the church's worship leader, suffered a stroke in the middle of the revival. He was thirty-three. This made no sense to me. Why would he suffer a stroke when he played such a pivotal role in a revival that involved so many youth? When he got out of the hospital and was recuperating at home, I stopped by after church to talk with him. I asked him if he could move his left hand. The stroke had affected his left side. He could move that hand, but with difficulty. I went home and prayed, "God, if you will let Fred play the piano tomorrow night in church, without pain, I will stand up and immediately announce my call to preach." (I wanted to make sure the previous two signs had not been coincidences.)

The next day I saw Fred again. He still could not move his hand normally, but he attended church that night. The church filled up with young people until no seats were left, and people were standing everywhere. I heard the piano begin to play and turned around. There was Fred playing the piano. I thought, *He's playing with one hand somehow.* But the music seemed too good for that.

After worship there was a spot left for one person to squeeze into, right in front of me. That was weird considering how full the church was. Fred sat down there, and I pecked him on the shoulder and said, "Fred, let me see you move your hand."

Fred lifted his hand up and moved it freely, not like he had shown me just half an hour earlier, before worship started.

I asked, "Fred, why did you decide to play the piano?"

He responded, "When I was sitting in the pew, I had a strong impression of hearing the Lord say to me, 'If you will try to play the piano, I will heal you.' So I went to the piano, and when I touched the keys, I was instantly healed."

My final question was, "Fred, did you have any pain?"

He responded, "No, none. All the pain left the moment I touched the keys."

I immediately stood up. When the pastor recognized me, I made good on my promise and announced my calling to become a preacher. It was November 22, 1970. Since the seventh grade, my plan had been to become a history teacher, but those plans were given up to fulfill God's call on my life. When I went to Oakland City College two months later, I majored in Religious Studies. I wanted to burn all bridges to anything but preaching.

My first day on campus, while I was buying textbooks, I also received a strong impression from God—one I have never forgotten, even now, forty-one years later. It was, "The issue of your lifetime will be the Holy Spirit."

That was a strange word for a Baptist student at a Baptist college. In response, the first book I bought after my required textbooks was *The Holy Spirit*. That impression would prove to be truly from God. Probably no other graduate of that college has seen more controversy over the Holy Spirit and His actions than I have.

I graduated from college in 1974 and from seminary in 1977. In 1982 I not only preached a series of sermons on healing, I prayed for the sick. Something happened at that point that almost derailed me from the healing ministry. A woman who pretended to be healed deceived me. She had fabricated her condition, and I did not discover it until after I let her testify in church to her healing. Then when she pretended another healing, I became suspicious. I found out the first healing was a fake. I was very hard on myself and backed away from healing, not preaching on it again for a year and a half. I was so disappointed in my own discernment, so embarrassed by being deceived, that I did not want to pray for anyone. But God had another plan.

Two things happened next that turned things around, culminating in a series of meetings that would forever change my life. That is not an overstatement—these things actually set the course for the rest of my life. First, I was in my office praying, "God, thank You that I'm not a liberal. I believe Jesus did what the Bible says He did. And thank You that I'm not a cessationist. I believe He still does what He did then."

I was expecting a "Well done, thou good and faithful servant with whom I am well pleased." But instead I heard from the Lord, "So what?"

"What do you mean, so what?" I quickly asked Him.

I heard, "You might as well be a liberal or a cessationist. It isn't enough to say you believe I still do what I did—if you don't know how to move in My gifts, you won't be able to do any more than a liberal or cessationist does."

This communication from the Spirit shook me. I determined right then that I would learn how to move in the gifts of the Holy Spirit.

Not long after this, the second life-changing event occurred. I invited a young man from my college to come preach for me. He did a fair enough job preaching on the woman with the issue of blood, but instead of preaching on healing, he spiritualized the text, giving it a nonhealing application. I had done the same many times. While listening, I began to have an experience with God that had nothing to do with the preacher or sermon. Hot tears rolled down my face, and I remember thinking, *What's going on? Why am I crying? This has nothing to do with the sermon.* (I later realized it was because of the visitation of the Holy Spirit.) I then heard the Lord strongly impress on me, "I want you to teach that I still heal today. I want you to have a conference on healing in this church. I want you to preach differently. No more three points and a poem. I want you to include more of My words in your sermon, and less of your own. I want you to preach a series of sermons on My works and My words—My ministry and My message."

The next day I spoke with Dr. Larry Hart of Oral Roberts University. I asked him if he would come hold a conference for me on healing. He told me that the best person he had ever heard at ORU for equipping people for healing was John Wimber. I had never heard of John Wimber, and I was not excited about inviting someone I had never heard to do the conference. The next morning, though, I saw John Wimber on TV and loved what I heard. Impressed, I called him. He told me he could not come, but could send a team in three months. I agreed, but asked him to make it six months so I could conclude my series on "The Words and Works of Jesus."

I began planning how to carry out the Lord's assignment to preach differently. I determined to look at all four gospels, try to reconstruct the chronology and include everything in the gospels in one series. I figured it would take about six months to preach through the material, and I also asked the church's deacons to come to an extra meeting with me each month to discuss the gifts of the Spirit and the baptism with the Spirit. My plan worked beautifully. I concluded those special meetings with the deacons and then taught my position—which all the deacons now understood and agreed with—to the church's home groups six weeks prior to our conference with the team from John's church.

In that preparation time, two more things happened of major importance in my experience of healing. First I went to Dallas and heard John Wimber in January 1984. For the first time in my life, I saw firsthand the power of God affecting people physically and causing them to tremble and/or fall. I was so excited. All I had seen prior to this was God's power touching someone emotionally. I had seen people cry under conviction for their sins or cry when touched by God's love after conversion. And as a child, I had once seen people laughing for joy in the Baptist church I grew up in. This was different.

During the meeting in Dallas, I had the opportunity to have John Wimber pray for me. I was afraid he might tell me everything wrong with my life through the gift of prophecy, but instead, he told me many highly encouraging things. What I remember most was when he said, "God says you are a Prince in the Kingdom of God."

Sometime later, John's vice president of Vineyard Ministries International told me that the first two times John and I had met, John had heard God tell him audibly that I would one day go around the world laying hands on pastors and leaders to impart and stir up spiritual gifts in them. John did not tell me this himself until shortly before he died. A few days after the outpouring began in Toronto, though, John did tell me that I was now starting on what God had shown him about me ten years earlier.

Second, a few weeks before the team from the Anaheim Vineyard Christian Fellowship arrived for our conference, I called ahead and spoke with Lance Pittluck. He had recently left the Presbyterian denomination and was being mentored as an intern there. I asked him if he could tell me anything that might increase our anointing for healing the sick. He asked if I believed in words of knowledge. That is a story in itself that I will tell you more about in chapter 10. Our whole phone conversation opened me up to a new realm of ministry I had never experienced before.

## The Healing Conference

When the conference began at my Baptist church, I was shocked by how many pastors and leaders came. We were packed out. I had written a letter to all the American Baptist pastors in Illinois, Wisconsin and Missouri; as well as all the Baptist, Methodist, Lutheran and other Evangelical pastors in southern Illinois, and some pastors in Missouri. The letter began, "If you, like me, are tired of going to the hospital and praying 'God, guide the surgeon's hand,' then I invite you to a conference on healing. I have invited people from the Anaheim Vineyard, who are seeing more healings and who can help us learn how to more effectively pray for the sick."

I will never forget my first impressions of that conference. The leader, Blaine Cook, was tremendously gifted with words of knowledge. He must have given about twenty the first morning. People came forward for prayer, and many were healed. The pastor of the First Baptist Church of Chillicothe, Illinois, fell at my wife's feet. He got up healed of a serious back injury from a car accident, removed the half-inch lift from his shoe and threw it away. The deaf heard, sight was greatly improved and many people were healed of pain.

Not only did healing occur, but impartation as well. Many people in my church were activated in gifts of healing, tongues

26

and words of knowledge. Many received a baptism with the Spirit, some became drunk in the Spirit and had to be driven home, many were seized with laughter, others fell into a state of peace, some had demons manifest and others received miraculous healings. I personally received an impartation that caused a major increase in words of knowledge and in healings. Several members of my congregation received an even stronger anointing than I did.

During my impartation, I felt electricity so strong that it caused me to shake. My wife received emotional healing, a physical healing and activation in words of knowledge. She fell to the floor under the power of God. This was something she had a great aversion to. If someone on Christian television happened to fall under the power, she would say, "If you believe that's real, you're the biggest fool I've ever met!" She did not believe it was real—that is, until it happened to her.

The next night, a young lady named Tammy Ferguson approached me and another man, John Gordon, for prayer. He had prayed for her in a previous service, but she needed more healing. She was born with spina bifida that caused her to lose control over her bladder, so she wore diapers at night. She also was hydrocephalic and had undergone twelve surgeries to put shunts into her head to drain fluid. We prayed, and Tammy was healed! She never had to wear diapers again. Neither did she ever need another shunt because now the fluid was flowing down into her spine normally. She was also healed of seizures, which she did not even tell us she was having. We did not pray about that, but she was healed of them anyway. She would not need to take eleven kinds of medicine for seizures anymore.

By September after the conference, I had resigned the pastorate at the Baptist church. I thought God had called me to go to a different city and plant a new church. Since I did not know where yet, I told some of the people who wanted a different kind of church that I would pastor them until I knew where to go. In about four months, I knew where I was called—St. Louis—but it took a whole year before I would begin work there. That year was like a sabbatical. With those people who were looking for something different, I started the first Vineyard in Illinois. We saw many healings, and I do not know if I have ever had a higher percentage of people who moved as powerfully in the gifts as the group who left the Baptist church to start the Vineyard with me.

One of the most memorable healings occurred on a Sunday night. My former associate pastor of the Baptist church, Tom Simpson, had come with me to start the Vineyard. He and his wife, Sandy, had both been activated in words of knowledge, had received the gift of tongues and were seeing people healed when they prayed. They were also activated in the gift of prophecy. On this particular Sunday, Tom had seen an open vision. (An open vision is different from seeing a mental picture. In an open vision, your field of vision is lost and you see the vision as if you are watching it on a large-screen TV.) In this open vision he saw a young boy, probably eleven or twelve, who was naked. The boy's muscles were withered on the left side. As Tom watched, the boy's right side began to wither as well.

Tom did not know what to do with this vision. He was confused about its interpretation. He did not know if it was a sign that the new church would wither and die, or if it should be interpreted literally rather than symbolically. Due to his confusion, he did not share the vision during our morning service. That afternoon, he and his siblings met at their parents' home with all the grandchildren. During this family day, the vision came to him again as an open vision. Again, he was confused by it. Then at the evening service, the vision came a third time. This time Tom came and told me the vision. He told me this was the third time it had come, and that he did not know how to interpret it. I related the vision to the church and asked if it made sense to anyone.

A woman who was visiting from the local Church of God (Anderson) said, "I know who that's for! It's for a boy who has a rare disease that is causing his muscles on the left side of his body to wither. He's supposed to go to the Shriners Hospital tomorrow for more testing. The prognosis is that the disease will gradually move to the right side and cause those muscles to wither also."

This woman called the boy's mother and asked her to put her hands on her son. We then prayed as a church for his healing. When he was examined the next day, the doctor said, "I don't know how to explain this, but the disease is gone. Not only is it not affecting the right side, but the left side muscles are being healed!"

That was just one of numerous healings we saw that year. From March 1984 until January 1986, the key leaders who helped me start that first Vineyard in Illinois drove to Texas four times to see either John Wimber or Blaine Cook. We also drove to Michigan, Ohio, northern Illinois and Nashville to learn more about how to move in the gifts of the Spirit and how to pray for the sick from the Vineyard leaders.

## The Grand Experiment

In January 1986 I resigned from the Vineyard church and took a job frying donuts in St. Louis so I would be in a position to start a new church there. From January until November,

29

I worked in 80 Kroger stores, training people in the bakery. I would drive to the St. Louis area and stay in a hotel on Sunday, then return home on Friday evenings. I made this 260-mile round trip every weekend. My wife, DeAnne, and our son, Josh, soon joined me and stayed in the hotel where I was staying. DeAnne was pregnant with Johannah, our second child, who would be born in July. We could not buy a house until our house in southern Illinois sold. In November, we finally bought a condo in the St. Louis area.

During those early days, I had to get up at 3:00 A.M. to fry donuts. I did not enjoy it. I was a night person and had often gone to bed at that time in the past—I did not like starting my day then! Because the job was so boring, and because I had been teaching that the lay people in my church should pray for people outside of church meetings, I looked for opportunities to pray for people at work.

I told God, "Lord, I am not going to preach anymore that people should pray for people at work if it doesn't work. I don't want to put a burden on them. This is going to be my grand experiment. I'm not going to tell anyone I'm a preacher. Instead, if You give me a word of knowledge, or if anyone says they're sick or I notice they're sick, I'm going to say to them, 'I'm a Christian. I've seen some people healed when I've prayed, but not everyone. I don't promise you anything, but if you'll let me, I'd like to pray for you.'"

The grand experiment worked! That year I saw more people healed in the Kroger grocery stores than I did in our church or house group meetings. Let me share with you one of the more memorable stories. I was working in the Kroger store in Centralia, Illinois. I noticed the head bakery clerk was quite nervous. After training her team, I was cleaning up my mess and washing the pans. When she came over, I said, "Don't be nervous. I don't work for Kroger, but for another company. I'm here as a technical representative to help you and your employees do a better job. So there's no need to be nervous."

She responded, "I'm nervous because I have a terrible ear infection, and my ear is so stopped up that I can only understand about half of what you're saying."

I said, "I'm a Christian. I've seen people healed when I prayed, though not always. I'd be glad to pray for you if you wish."

"I'd like that," she said. I asked her when she would like prayer, and she replied, "Right now would be good."

We went back into the "holy of holies" where the cloud of smoke filled the room (which interpreted means the break room full of cigarette smoke). We sat down, and I said, "No one will even know we're praying. I'll pray with my eyes open, and you don't have to close yours. People will think we're talking. If you feel anything happen, I want you to tell me."

When I began to pray, she closed her eyes anyway. I prayed, "Lord, I bless Jane's ear (not her real name) and command it to open."

Immediately she opened her eyes and looked at me, startled.

I said, "Your ear just opened, didn't it?"

Jane had tears in her eyes. I could tell she was shocked. She replied, "The moment you commanded my ear to open, it did, and I can now hear very clearly."

I was actually surprised by how quickly she had been healed. I asked her how this made her feel. I also asked her if she was a Christian.

She replied, "I used to go to church and was even in leadership. But I was hurt in church years ago, and since then I haven't gone."

I asked, "But now that God has healed your ear, how do you feel about Him?" Then I told her she should find a good church to attend. She told me she would do that. This head bakery clerk had been apprehended by the power of God.

We returned to the bakery. I was finishing washing the pans when my ear clogged up. This was sudden and very strange. I feel words of knowledge, so I turned to Jane and asked, "Did your ear just clog up again?"

She answered, "Yes! How did you know?"

I told her sometimes I know what God wants to do by feeling the problem someone else has. This time I knew the problem was not a natural infection of the ear, but was caused by an afflicting spirit. I asked her if we could pray again. She said yes. I asked, "Where can we pray?"

"In the walk-in freezer," she said.

We went into the freezer and I prayed, commanding the afflicting spirit to leave her ear. She began to tremble. I was not sure if it was the Spirit of God or the coldness of the freezer. However, her pain left. And soon I was finished and left the store.

A few months later, I returned to the store to train again. When I saw Jane, she told me she had rededicated her life to God and had found a church to join. Also, she added, her ear infection had never come back.

I could tell many more stories of people healed in the Kroger stores. No one ever refused my offer to pray for healing, and almost every person I prayed for was not attending church. Most were not Christians, yet I was amazed by how receptive they were to prayer.

It was a different situation in the home meetings and Sunday celebration meetings of the church. Some people were healed, but many were not. I struggled with this odd situation. I felt as though something was wrong with this picture. Why was it easier to see healing among the "believing unbelievers" than among the "unbelieving believers"?

The answer to that question is the basis of chapter 4 ahead, "Unbelieving Believers and Believing Unbelievers," in which I identify the source of the problem and suggest some factors that have contributed to the demise of people's faith in healing. Before we move on, though, let's hear from Bill about how God led him into the ministry of revival and healing.

# 2

# BILL'S JOURNEY

*Bill*

I am a fifth-generation pastor on my dad's side of the family, fourth on my mom's. My three children are now the sixth generation of pastors. I grew up in a very good Christian home and had a fear of God. Forgiveness of sin was appealing to me, almost to the same degree that hell was unappealing. And while I never lived in out-and-out rebellion, neither was I known as a passionate follower of Jesus.

The thought of becoming a pastor never once entered my mind. I did not care for crowds, and speaking in front of people was frightening. My parents never talked with me about that option for my life, either. They thought my brother might become a pastor, but not me. Their goal for me was that I would make it to heaven.

At the end of my high school years, I moved from the Los Angeles area to Redding, California, where my parents became the pastors of Bethel Church. The Jesus People movement and the charismatic movement were in full swing at that point. The year was 1968.

In 1970 things started to break loose in the Redding church as the Holy Spirit began to move powerfully. Many guest speakers came to us during this season. I was stirred each time, but never as much as when Mario Murillo would come. He had attended junior college in Redding before our arrival, which endeared him to the city. Plus my dad became a great personal friend and an encouragement to him—so much so that Mario was the one I asked to speak at my dad's funeral in 2004. He referred to my dad as his "compass."

Mario's message was simple: Be absolutely abandoned to Christ. He provoked me in all the right ways. I never missed a meeting when he was in town. Even though I had not "jumped in all the way" yet, he spoke to something deep within me. One Saturday night, alone, I finally said yes to God—the absolute yes. For me, everything changed that night. I showed up the next Sunday morning with Bible and notebook in hand, ready to learn. I began to devour the Scriptures, along with other books, especially books on prayer. My friend and youth pastor, Chip Worthington, fed me with an endless supply. It was actually those books that created a hunger in me for the Word of God. When I read different authors' insights, I thought, *I must study the Bible, too, and learn to get what they get.* I had known in my head that God talks to people through His Word, but now I was learning it in my heart.

## Normal versus Special

I loved to see Mario Murillo in action. He preached with such power. Miracles often took place in his meetings. The greatest, of course, were mass conversions. But miracles of healing were normal, too. His words of knowledge were the most amazing thing I had ever seen. Once I saw him point to a woman and say, "You have a tumor right here in your stomach," pointing to that location on his own abdomen. He then told her that she had not even told her husband, but if she would put her hand where the tumor was, she would find out it was gone. She began to weep as she discovered that her "secret tumor" was indeed gone. Needless to say, she was overcome by God's love and power.

Mario became an example to me. He was closer to me in age than some of the other ministers I had seen, and it was the crowd at his meetings who convinced me I could give my all to Jesus. They were mostly young people who loved Jesus with all of their hearts. They exerted a godly peer pressure. Because of the example of others around me, it became obvious to me that I could love God with all my heart. But I also knew a lifestyle of miracles was out of my reach. I knew Mario was a very special instrument of God, whereas I was normal—and therefore unqualified for such a lifestyle.

I also saw Kathryn Kuhlman on several occasions, an absolutely wonderful experience. But I knew that she, too, was very special to God. Her experiences were powerful and unique, which signified to me that the anointing she carried was only for special people.

A hunger for a gospel of power was deeply embedded in me, in spite of my misconceptions of the ministry of power. The seeds were actually planted in me much earlier in life. My maternal grandparents lived with us most of my life. They were baptized in the Holy Spirit in 1901 and 1903. Miracles were normal for them, and they told me stories. They had spent considerable time receiving from Aimee Semple McPherson's ministry. In fact, my grandfather did all kinds of special painting work in her home. As well as doing regular house painting, he was a real artist known for his special designs on ceilings and the like. He painted during and between pastorates.

My grandparents also sat under Smith Wigglesworth's ministry. Grandpa loved to tell me about those days, but he would add, "Not everyone loved Wigglesworth." Smith was very bold in his pursuit of God and his hatred of disease. Of course, he is well loved today—because he is dead. He cannot offend anyone with his extreme pursuit of pleasing God with his faith now. Israel loved all her dead prophets, too.

To my way of thinking, these ministers who were examples to me were extraordinary, whereas nothing qualified me for a life of miracles. I was uneducated—no Bible school, no seminary, not even much college training. I was a poor student, and as a result, I lacked many of the practical disciplines that others my age characteristically displayed. I could not speak in front of crowds, and quite frankly, did not want to. But I did say the ultimate yes to God, so that meant anything could be required of me, which was okay. Preaching just could not originate from me as a goal. It was not in me.

But more important to me than the lack of education or mentoring in the supernatural was that I had never had what I will refer to as a power encounter with God. Almost everyone I had ever heard of who had a miracle ministry could take you back to the time when they experienced their special moment with God. It was in that encounter with God that *the call of God* was given to them. I had never experienced anything like that. Nothing close. I was thankful for the still, small voice and thankful that He would speak to me from His Word. Yet there was nothing seemingly spectacular about my relationship with God. Even so, I would occasionally pray for the sick or even try to prophesy. But nothing significant ever happened. I tried hard to hear from God in a supernatural way, but still nothing. Yet I loved Him so much, and worship flowed from me unforced.

## Discovering a Heart to Pastor

Under the leadership of Chip Worthington, we started a street ministry in Redding to minister to the youth of our city, as well as to some of the hippies traveling the West Coast. We also served as a discipleship ministry for the Jesus People movement. I lived in what we called the Salt House, a ministry center that provided Bible studies and outreaches for young people. I rose early and retired late in the day just to pray. The time spent in prayer was impressive, but the prayers were mostly about me. Spiritual children, like natural children, are quite self-absorbed. I know God valued my sincere zeal to be like Christ. It would take a bit of time for me to learn that transformation does not happen by becoming inwardly focused.

So many tormented and demonized people were hitchhiking around the country at that time, and it seemed as if they all stopped by our place. I tried hard to bring deliverance. The only person I remember getting freed received prayer from Chip and his wife, Linda, in a side room while ten or fifteen of us interceded in the living room. I did not realize at that time that when our experience does not match what the Bible promises, the lack is not on God's side of the equation. Our awareness of lack is usually what He uses to summon us into a deeper experience with Him. From that deeper experience true power flows.

My years at the Salt House made me aware of my heart for people and my desire to learn and teach. It took a while for me to admit it, but I realized that I had a pastor's heart. No one was more surprised at the discovery than me. I soon took on other responsibilities that gave me a chance to find out just what I was called to do. Most of the responsibilities were in areas I was none too good at, but Bethel Church needed help and I was happy to try.

I was invited to pastor Mountain Chapel in Weaverville, California, in 1978. I told my dad, our senior pastor in Redding, that I would not accept such an invitation on the basis of it being a promotion. That had no appeal to me. The only important thing was to know that this was God's assignment and have the leadership in Redding recognize it and send me and my family—which they did. We served in Weaverville for seventeen wonderful years.

Reading John G. Lake furthered my quest along the way. His insights into the Spirit-filled life are the greatest I have seen anywhere. His insights and stories ruined me. But I still could not get past the feelings of inadequacy. My many prayers for others seemed to confirm that I was not qualified for miracles. Nothing ever happened.

Still, the thought of miracles as a part of the Gospel would not leave me. Miracles were in the Scriptures. I struggled with the idea that I did not qualify to be involved in them. But the cry in my heart for a more powerful expression of the Gospel finally got louder than my cry of inadequacy. Sometimes we need to fear lack more than fearing excess if we really want a breakthrough.

As I already mentioned, the one thing that had become the anchor of my walk with the Lord was that I was a worshiper. My dad had taught us on worship many years earlier, and I remember bowing my head to pray after he taught us the ministry of the inner court versus the ministry of the outer court. I prayed, "God, I give You the rest of my life to teach me how to minister to You."

The presence of the Lord was so strong on us as a church family when we were in Weaverville. We extended our times of worshiping and glorifying God in our services and prayer meetings. As a result, we became familiar with the anointing of the Holy Spirit. That connection to the presence would later serve as a primary building block in my learning how the Holy Spirit moves in other contexts like healing and prophecy.

## Major Download

The greatest breakthrough in ministry for me came in 1987, when I attended two conferences put on by John Wimber. The first one actually discouraged me somewhat. I have attended many wonderful conferences through the years, but for the first time ever, at that one I heard nothing new. It was a divine setup. Every teaching I heard that week I had already done before, right down to some of the illustrations. That was strange. I had thought the illustrations were my own. The discouraging part drove me into a measure of breakthrough—I left with the realization that I had good theology, but those speakers had experience for what they believed.

At no time during Wimber's conference did he lay hands on people for impartation, but something was still imparted to us. When I got home, I knew it was time for me to "put a demand" on what I believed. My risk factor had to line up with the boldness of my beliefs, and unbeknownst to me, I had come home with a greater courage to take risks. So I did, and an immediate change came in my ministry.

Everything was now different. I decided to teach a midweek class on healing. While I knew I was not an expert in the slightest possible way, I also knew you get what you preach. We watched videos and tried to copy what we saw. The ministers on the videos were as diverse in nature as you could get: Charles and Francis Hunter, John Wimber and Mario Murillo. If we knew of someone with an anointing in healing, we would copy them. I remember reading a story from a famous musician who said that his efforts to be completely original in writing music had failed until he returned to studying what had already been written by other seasoned musicians. Sometimes copying others is the way we find out how our gift works.

For the first time in my Christian walk, I saw miracles start to happen in our church. It was dramatic and exciting. This is what I had read about that had always seemed to happen long ago or far away. Now it was happening to me! And it was almost without fanfare. It seemed I had discovered a key that made the impossible possible, but I could not have told you what it was. I just knew things were different. While I had never had the "call of God" encounter that others had, I did have the command of Scripture to "heal the sick" (Matthew 10:8). And that was enough.

The first major miracle God used me in was actually in a public place, a store in which I knew the owner. He told me he would be forced to retire because his arthritis was so bad. He could no longer use his tools or reach for boxes on his shelves. Others were in the store when we talked, so I did not feel I could pray for him then. I came back to see him another time when the store was empty. With just the two of us present, he again brought up his affliction. This time I told him that I thought God wanted to heal him and asked if I could pray. He agreed. I laid my hands on his hands and elbows, invited the Holy Spirit to come (as John Wimber modeled) and commanded the arthritis to leave. It did. The store owner was shocked—completely shocked. So was I! That was the beginning of the breakthrough.

### The Toronto Effect

Others began getting healed. Sometimes people fell under God's power when I prayed for them. That had never happened before. Ever. I was most encouraged because those receiving healing included children. Healing poured out onto the streets of our city. One of the most powerful meetings I have ever been in to date involved a few dozen children ranging in age from five to twelve. The Holy Spirit came in such power that one eight-year-old boy lost the ability to speak for several hours. His mom called us somewhat panicked, asking what had happened. She said he would weep whenever the name of Jesus was mentioned. I told her God was touching her son and to just watch what God was doing. The boy's speechlessness only lasted for one night, but it marked him forever.

This outpouring of the Holy Spirit would come and go over the next nine years—from 1987 to 1995. I did not know how to keep it burning or help it grow. I did not realize then that it was always God who lit the fire on the altar, but it was the priests who kept it burning—that all revivals start because of God, but end because of man. It never occurred to me that I had a role in maintaining and increasing a move of God. Somehow I thought things ended out of God's sovereign choice. Since then, I have learned that the sovereignty of God gets blamed for the end of many great things.

Our church family grew in the anointing for healing and various kinds of Holy Spirit ministry. Worship became even more powerful. The prophetic nature of the church dramatically increased as well, largely because of Kris Vallotton, who had started to come into his own in the prophetic call of God on his life.

I heard that God also was moving powerfully in a church in Toronto, Canada. I made arrangements to visit in February 1995. What I saw overwhelmed me. Most everything I saw had happened in our church back in 1987, too, but it is quite different to see God move powerfully over thousands as compared to a smaller group. It was sensory overload.

When I closed my eyes, I was able to recognize that it was the same Holy Spirit we had seen move powerfully in our midst in Weaverville. Throughout my days in Toronto, I followed the exercise of closing my eyes to block out what I saw and rediscovering the presence that filled the room. Sometimes we see more with our eyes closed.

On my way to Toronto, I had prayed, "God, if You will touch me again, I will never change the subject. I will not add what You're doing to what we're doing. I will make what You're doing the only thing we do." That prayer came out of the realization that some things end only because we do not become the person He needs us to be in order to give increase to us. I wanted increase, and I received prayer every time there was an opportunity in Toronto. In fact, I got prayer five times the first night. I jokingly tell people they could have had an altar call for African-American, pregnant pastors' wives and I would have gone forward. It is close to the truth. I *had* to have God touch me again.

For all the praying over me, nothing major happened to me that week—at least nothing I noticed. I had heard stories of profound encounters with God others had experienced in their Toronto visits. It seemed like many thousands were touched powerfully. Even without that experience, I was still thankful. I knew I was in the middle of something I had only read about before.

Although I had now seen God move powerfully at home and had even seen a few miracles, I knew there was so much more. A holy dissatisfaction possessed my soul. Mario Murillo told me recently that in the same way that Hannah's barrenness was used by God to make her desperate for a breakthrough, a child (see 1 Samuel 1), so God used my spiritual barrenness to ignite a passion in me for the impossible. That kind of passion qualified and prepared Hannah for her child, and in the same way, it prepared me for the very thing I longed for. I believe Mario was right. God shaped me through hunger. Proverbs 27:7 says, "A sated man loathes honey, but to a famished man any bitter thing is sweet." Many people miss out on a move of God because they are not hungry enough. Only the desperate think that an imperfect, incomplete move of God is wonderful. Starving people think a crust of bread is a meal. Most seem to want a move of God without problems or messes. Moves of God just do not come that way.

## Embracing the Subtle—and Beyond

During my days in Toronto, the presence of God was so sweet, so peaceful. While others seemed to encounter Him almost violently, my experience seemed almost uneventful by comparison. But it was real, and it was enough. Some answers come in seed form—"a cloud as small as a man's hand" (1 Kings 18:44). I thanked God and told Him that I would gladly give up my life for the outpouring of the Spirit.

On my return home, the outpouring started almost immediately. Yet it was a subtle increase, almost like my experience in Toronto. I began to cry out to God day and night for eight months. My prayer was, "God, I want more of You at any cost! I will pay any price!" I would even wake myself up praying—not wake up to pray, but wake up praying. There was such a pull in my heart for more. This was Hannah's burden for the impossible—an inexplicable burden and somewhat hard to manage.

In October 1995, I had an encounter with God that would mark me for life. Dick Joyce, a dear friend and prophet, was ministering in our church in Weaverville. We had traveled to Toronto together. Although he had already been ministering in great power for years, the experience there brought a freshness to him as well. The meetings he had with us were wild. It was Toronto in the mountains of California. People's lives were being transformed quickly and dramatically all over the room. One night I got to bed quite late, as is the norm during these times. And in a moment, I went from a dead sleep to being as wide awake as you can imagine, with what felt like a thousand volts of electricity pulsating through my body. I looked at the clock and it was 3:00 A.M. exactly. Interestingly, I had prayed for a friend that night and told him that I felt God was going to surprise him, which could happen in the middle of the day or middle of the night. I had said it could come at 3:00 in the morning. As soon as I saw the clock, I remembered saying it and said, "God, You set me up!" My arms and legs shot out in silent explosions as this power seemed released through my hands and feet. The more I tried to stop it, the more intense it got. I actually thought that this power had "blown a fuse" in my body and that I might never recover. It sounds strange to say it now, but that was my fear in the moment.

Some of the most important things that happen to us are the most difficult to explain to others, yet they are undeniably from God. I was embarrassed in this experience and felt my face turn red. I had no control over my body. My head could turn side to side, but that was it. It was glorious, but not pleasant.

As this uncontrollable electric force flowed through my body, certain scenes came to mind. The first was of me trying to speak to our church family in this condition and realizing that no one would believe this was from God. The next picture I saw was of me in front of my favorite restaurant in town. The whole town would laugh at me. I looked as though I had serious physical and emotional problems. Then I remembered that Jacob wrestled with an angel and limped the rest of his life. Mary had an encounter that not even Joseph believed was from God. An angel had to convince him that the Spirit of God had truly come upon her and that she would bear the Christ child. Mary bore the stigma of "mother of an illegitimate child" all her days. Interestingly, Scripture calls her *highly favored*. But sometimes favor from heaven causes problems on earth.

I truly wondered if I would ever function as a normal human being again. It seemed like if I said yes to God in that experience, I actually might have to stay in bed the rest of my life. Tears streamed down the sides of my face as He showed me "the price" for more. I gladly yielded, crying, *More, God. More! I must have more of You at any cost! If I lose respectability and get You in the exchange, I'll gladly make that trade. Just give me more of You!*

The power surges did not stop. They continued throughout the night, with me weeping and praying, *More, Lord, more. Please give me more of You.* Then at 6:38 A.M. it all stopped. I got out of bed completely refreshed. This experience continued the following two nights, beginning moments after I got into bed.

None of my friends would have said fear of man was a problem for me. I had made some tough choices in ministry through the years that showed I feared God instead of man. But God could see what really needed to change in me in order for me to be trusted with the *more* I had asked for. Little did I know what was in store for me and my family in the coming months. That yes to God made what followed much easier.


## Bethel Church and Randy Clark

Bethel Church of Redding, California, the church that had sent us out to Weaverville, was without a pastor. The people asked us to come back to our "mother church." This was only a few months after that 3:00 A.M. encounter. The leadership wanted us to come because of their hunger for revival, and they had heard of the outpouring at Mountain Chapel. We accepted the invitation with this condition: I was born for revival—this was not negotiable. Revival had to be in the hearts of the people, with unanimous support from the leadership. They said yes.

The outpouring when we came to Bethel began almost immediately. But it started small, almost in seed form again. The church was tired from their eight months without a pastor. I asked everyone to come to the front of the church on a Sunday night to pray. I invited the Holy Spirit to come with power upon them, and He did. He fell powerfully on one person. My wife, Beni, and I looked at each other and said, "We've got it. Now no one can stop it!"

Sometimes we wait for things to mature and become fully grown before acknowledging them for what they are. An apple just beginning to grow is as much an apple as is one ready to eat. It just lacks time. If we will give honor to things in their infant stages, we will see more things grow to maturity. The Scripture says not to despise the day of small beginnings, for the Lord rejoices to see a work begin (see Zechariah 4:10).

This outpouring increased greatly over the following weeks. Healing became a normal part of it. Numerous miracles and deliverances took place during worship or during the Toronto-style ministry time. One man was frustrated during the Sunday morning message because his Bible appeared so blurry. When he got home he removed his glasses, only to find he had been healed and did not need them anymore.

Another woman had esophageal cancer. During worship her hands got hot. She took it as a sign and told her husband that God had just healed her. When she went to the doctor, he told her that her kind of cancer does not go away. But on examining her, he found that not only was there no cancer—she also had a new esophagus.

These kinds of things started happening with regularity. At one time we had six cases of cancer or tumors disappear in eight weeks. That was huge for us, especially considering that we were not focusing on healing. We began to realize that some of the things we work so hard for actually come with the presence. Making room for God to do as He pleases and then cooperating with Him is the greatest thing we can do to see an increase in signs and wonders.

Randy Clark, my co-author, would become key in where our church was going in this move of God. I had seen him many times in Toronto videos, but I had never heard him before in person. I knew I had to meet him, and a mutual friend arranged for us to do so when Beni and I flew to one of his conferences. We had a twenty-minute meeting with Randy before his dinner appointment with one of the speakers. I told him I wanted the anointing that was on his life. He mentioned that there would be an impartation service the last night of the conference. I also told him of the miracles we were seeing and that we would love for him to come to Redding. He agreed.

The last night of that conference was a wonderful time of impartation. After Randy laid his hands on me, I spent considerable time on the floor, soaking in God's presence, asking for God to go deeper in me. God promised to work beyond our imagination and beyond our prayers, but all "according to the power that works within us" (Ephesians 3:20). For Him to work consistently beyond the reach of our prayers and imagination, we must allow Him to work *deep* within us.

Randy came to Redding for four days in 1997. Before he came, miracles had become weekly occurrences, but during the four days he was with us over four hundred people were healed. It was the largest number he had ever seen happen in the United States during the same period of time. A deposit had been made—one that set a course for our church and eventually for our ministry school.

## Today

Healings and miracles have become normal today. I rejoice in this. A majority of them happen in public. While Jesus did not heal everyone alive in His time, He did heal everyone who came to Him. His is the only standard worth following.

Because we have developed a reputation in the area of miracles, people fly into Redding weekly, hoping that God will touch them. Sometimes several hundred visit Bethel, all with great needs. I am happy to report that many leave well and whole. But many others leave in the same condition in which they came. I refuse to blame God for this, as though He has a purpose in their disease. And I refuse to lower the standard of Scripture to my level of experience so I can feel good about myself. I am not looking to feel good about myself. I am looking to be like Jesus. I must accurately represent Him until I can accurately *re-present* Him. And finally, I will not allow guilt or shame to run my life because of an apparent lack on my side of the equation. Becoming "self focused" works against the anointing He puts upon us to touch others with His grace.

Healing is often said to be mysterious. I agree. But Jesus is not complicated. He made His will quite simple, saying "on earth as it is in Heaven" (Matthew 6:10). When people come to me for healing and they leave the same way they came, I pray like this: *Father, they came to me expecting to encounter Jesus, and all they got was me. And neither of us is impressed. You've got to work deeper in me so that when the multitudes come to us, they get more than a Bill encounter.*

We started in all of this by crying out to God in private and taking risks in public. Those are essentials in healing, and they have never changed through the years. Taking personal responsibility to do the impossible is the only way I can honestly face my responsibility to represent Jesus. In Matthew 10:8, Jesus did not command us to *pray* for the sick. He commanded us to *heal* them.

# Part 2

# A THEOLOGY OF HEALING

The ministry of healing is based on solid scriptural and theological foundations, both past and present. We look closely at the biblical truths and theological basis for believing that the gifts of healing demonstrate the good news of God's Kingdom for today. We also discuss numerous insights on healing that have been well presented by others from the time of the early Church through the last century, as well as adding some new insights of our own.

# 3

# THE GIFTS OF THE SPIRIT TODAY

## *Randy*

One day my wife, DeAnne, was praying for our son Joshua. He was only about three at the time, and he was having an asthma attack. She was praying with real seriousness because we had almost lost him to such an attack already—at least that is what the asthma department's nurse specialist at St. Louis's Children's Hospital told us. That time his lips turned blue, and he lost control of his bladder. The nurse told us the next thing was cardiac arrest. From then on, we took asthma attacks very seriously. For years we would be awakened at 3:00 A.M. with Josh in another attack.

On this day, he looked up at DeAnne and said, "Don't pray that way, Mommy. Pray the other way!"

She asked, "What do you mean?"

Josh replied, "You know, Mommy—when you use words I don't understand."

DeAnne responded, "Why, Josh?"

He replied, "Because it works better."

About thirteen years later, I experienced my first creative miracle when a woman who had advanced Parkinson's disease was healed. Since I was away from home, I called DeAnne the next morning to tell her about this miracle. Before I could say anything, she asked, "You had something very powerful happen last night, didn't you?"

I said, "Yes, an amazing miracle. But how did you know?"

DeAnne replied, "Did it happen around midnight?"

"Yes, it did!" I answered. "How did you know?"

DeAnne proceeded to tell me about her experience with our youngest son, Jeremiah, who was between one and two at the time. About midnight he had woken up screaming, acting as if he had a terrible earache. DeAnne was up till 5:00 A.M. with him. She told me that as long as she prayed in tongues he would not cry, but the moment she switched to praying in English, the pain would become so bad that he would begin crying again.

More than once when we have experienced a major spiritual breakthrough, a counterattack of some sort has come against us. Spiritual warfare is real, and as a family we are always prepared to fight it through. This was why Jeremiah's earache clued DeAnne in to the possibility that I had seen a major healing. This was the only earache he ever had growing up!

These two stories are not theological or biblical arguments for the existence of tongues today, and I am not trying to get anyone to speak in tongues. The purpose was to give you a practical, not theological, value for a gift of the Spirit and to indicate how beneficial the gift has been to my wife and sons. I do not believe you have to speak in tongues to be filled or baptized with the Holy Spirit, but I believe this gift has practical applications. I have spoken in tongues for almost forty years now, and I have found it a useful gift that helps me with life and its problems.

Bottom line, in this chapter I contend for an understanding of the gifts as the blessing of God's power to help us in life. They are signs of the inbreak of His Kingdom, and they help to establish His domain by pushing back the powers of darkness, sickness and the demonic. An "inbreak of the Kingdom" is when the power of God is released in the earth to perform a sign, wonder, healing or miracle. It is the Holy Spirit manifesting the Kingdom of God in the earth, and it is a specific example of when the "strong man's house is being plundered" due to Jesus defeating the devil through His crucifixion, resurrection, ascension and pouring out of the Spirit.

The issue before us here is whether or not the sign gifts—meaning tongues, the interpretation of tongues, prophecy, gifts of healing, and the working of miracles—are still in existence. Many question theologically whether or not the sign gifts are meant to be active and available to Christians today. Obviously, due to my opening two stories, I believe they are. They have great value, as do the other gifts of the Spirit.

One way of clarifying this issue is to ask whether the sign gifts are for *evidential* purposes or *beneficial* purposes. Are they supposed to authenticate the message of apostles, or are they supposed to help people as part of the Good News itself? Put another way, *do they prove the Gospel or express the Gospel? Do they authenticate correct doctrine or reveal the mercy of God?*

I believe these gifts are part of the Gospel and are meant to show that the Kingdom of God is at hand. Given to reveal God's mercy and love for His people, they are meant more as a benefit to us than as evidence of correct doctrine. I believe they are demonstrations of God's grace and His divine enablements.

Many Christians were taught *not* to believe the sign gifts are for today. Why? Because their pastors were either trained as liberals not to believe in the supernatural—period—or they were trained as cessationists to believe that God stopped the occurrence of miracles after the Bible was canonized. This latter viewpoint is based on the understanding that the purpose of miracles was to give credit to the writing of the apostles as evidence, vindicating the Bible because the miracles existed in the lives of the apostles who wrote the Bible. The problem with this viewpoint is that so much of the New Testament was not written by the apostles, and so many apostles did not write any Scripture at all. Therefore, validating the writing of the apostles by means of evidential miracles does not make sense since it only covers a little more than half the Scripture written, as shown in an email Dr. Jon Ruthven sent me after he researched the authorship of the New Testament. To determine what portion was written by the apostles, he went to the Greek text of the New Testament and stripped out all verse numbers, English titles and so on, leaving only the raw text. Making the most conservative attributions—counting Matthew, the Pastoral Epistles and Revelation all as "apostolic" or written directly by the apostles—here are his results:

- The apostles wrote 81,628 words or 59 percent of the New Testament.
- Non-apostles wrote 56,392 words or 41 percent of the New Testament.

Dr. Ruthven wondered, as I do, why out of the 89 or so apostles listed in the New Testament (counting the 72 referred to in Luke 10 who were "apostled" in verb form), why only 3 or 4 wrote Scripture if Scripture writing were their main job? Why, for that matter, was such a high percentage of the New Testament authorship entrusted to non-apostles?

I suggest that the purpose of miracles and healings was not evidential or meant to back up the apostles' writings. The Scriptures themselves do not teach that it was, nor does the formation of the New Testament bear up this teaching. Miracles and healings came because once again God heard the cry of His people and came down to rescue them from their taskmasters—not Egyptian taskmasters this time, but the demonic and the disease that Jesus came to free people from, all who were "oppressed by the devil" (Acts 10:38, NKJV). This is why in his book *The Miracle Stories of the Gospels*, British New Testament scholar Alan Richardson affirmed years ago that "miracles of healing are, as it were, symbolic demonstrations of God's forgiveness in action" (SCM Press, 1941, 61–62).

In the pages of this chapter, we will study Scripture to determine three things. One, do the Scriptures teach that the sign gifts are perpetual and are to continue until Jesus returns, or were these gifts expected to end with the death of the apostles or the completion of the Bible? Two, how important is power to the actual preaching of the Gospel? And three, were the apostles the only ones in the New Testament who worked signs and miracles? Let's be good Bereans (again, see Acts 17:11) and study what the Bible teaches about these things.

As a side note for those who are interested in reading about the operation and application of the gifts immediately, Part 3 of this book, "The Practice of Healing," will get into the specific "how-tos" of healing. If that group includes you, you might want to jump ahead to Part 3 right now and learn more about the practical aspects of these gifts. You can see how ministry in the gifts works first, then come back to this important chapter and the next later. In these pages just ahead, I lay a foundation to show the biblical basis of healing and also show historically how the Church has shifted away from a scriptural view of the sign gifts—with the result being the formation of so many unbelieving believers. Examining Scripture on the one hand and Church history on the other will help us shift our thinking back to where it should be. We can recover our faith in healing and realize that the sign gifts are intended for us today and every day until the Second Coming of Jesus.

## The Gifts Are Perpetual

Let's look first at the Scriptures that seem to indicate that the gifts—all of them—are to continue until Jesus returns and consummates His Kingdom on earth.

Matthew 28:18–20 is an important one:

> Then Jesus came to them and said, "All authority in heaven and on earth has been given to me. Therefore go and make disciples of all nations, baptizing them in the name of the Father and of the Son and of the Holy Spirit, and teaching them to obey everything I have commanded you. And surely I am with you always, to the very end of the age."

This passage indicates that people who become Christians should be taught to do what Jesus taught the disciples to do. Healing the sick and casting out demons top the list, and nothing indicates that those were only meant to be done until the Bible was canonized. As long as we baptize in the name of the Father, the Son and the Holy Spirit, we are to continue teaching the newly baptized to heal the sick and cast out demons.

The Kingdom of heaven parables Jesus told in Matthew 13 seem to mitigate against the view of dispensationalism that sees the end-time church as lukewarm instead of victorious. Every parable—the sower and the seed, the mustard seed and especially the yeast and dough—teaches the ongoing increase of the Kingdom of God. Nowhere do they indicate that the Kingdom will start out with power and great growth, but will sputter and lose its energies of grace—the gifts of the Spirit.

Romans 11:29 clearly teaches that "God's gifts and his call are irrevocable"—the opposite of cessationism. The King James Version says they are "without repentance," meaning God does not change His mind, first giving them and then taking them back. First Corinthians 1:7 says, "Therefore you do not lack any spiritual gift as you eagerly wait for our Lord Jesus Christ to be revealed." Since Paul said the Christians were not to lack "any" gift as they waited for the revelation of Jesus Christ, this is clear scriptural evidence for believing in the continuation of the gifts until Jesus comes again.

First Corinthians 13:10 says, "but when perfection comes, the imperfect disappears." It amazes me that this verse is used by both cessationists and noncessationists. Cessationists say the coming of "perfection" refers to the completion of the Bible. Noncessationists, along with the unanimous testimony of the early Church fathers, say "perfection" refers to the Second Coming of Jesus.

Ephesians 3:14–21 is a passage written to Christians who have already repented and been baptized into Christ, and who have received the Holy Spirit. He came into them and gave them life:

> For this reason I kneel before the Father, from whom his whole family in heaven and on earth derives its name. I pray that out of his glorious riches he may strengthen you with power through his Spirit in your inner being, so that Christ may dwell in your hearts through faith. And I pray that you, being rooted and established in love, may have power, together with all the saints, to grasp how wide and long and high and deep is the love of Christ, and to know this love that surpasses

knowledge—that you may be filled to the measure of all the fullness of God.

Now to him who is able to do immeasurably more than all we ask or imagine, according to his power that is at work within us, to him be glory in the church and in Christ Jesus throughout all generations, for ever and ever! Amen.

Paul prays that God may strengthen believers with power through His Spirit in their inner being. He wants Christians to have "power" and be "filled to the measure of all the fullness of God." Indispensable for such an experience is to "know the love that surpasses knowledge" (verses 18–19). How could we be filled to the fullness of God if He removed part of His grace gifts? Would we not be less than full if He took something of Himself, His energies and His gifts from us?

Paul's understanding of God's ability to work on our behalf is amazing. First, God can do "immeasurably more than all we ask or imagine," and second, this doing is "according to His power that is at work within us" (verse 20). The primary way God reveals His power through us is in our exercise of faith by *hearing* His directives and *obeying* them. Hearing and obeying are largely (though not entirely) contingent upon the operation of the gifts. Third, this will bring Him glory, and fourth, this glory is to be unto Him both in the Church and in Christ Jesus. How long should we expect this situation to occur in the Church and in Christ Jesus? Till we have the complete Bible? No! We are to expect this power to bring Him glory "throughout all generations, forever and ever!" (verse 21).

When you understand that to Paul, *glory* and *power* were synonymous, and that the number one way God received glory in the Bible was through signs and wonders, miracles and healings, it causes you to see the necessity of all the gifts continuing until Jesus returns. John also expressed the relationship between *power* and *glory* in John 2:11 when he talked about Jesus' miracle at Cana: "This, the first of his miraculous signs, Jesus performed at Cana in Galilee. He thus revealed his glory, and his disciples put their faith in him." I did a word study in this area and discovered that healings, miracles, signs and wonders were indeed the number one way God received glory or glorified His name.

Ephesians 4:7–13 tells us both the duration and the purpose of the office gifts:

> But to each one of us grace has been given as Christ appor-tioned it. This is why it says: "When he ascended on high, he led captives in his train and gave gifts to men." . . . It was he who gave some to be apostles, some to be prophets, some to be evangelists, and some to be pastors and teachers, to prepare God's people for works of service, so that the body of Christ may be built up *until we all reach unity in the faith and in the knowledge of the Son of God and become mature, attaining to the whole measure of the fullness of Christ* [emphasis added].

This passage teaches that the office gifts of apostles, prophets, evangelists, pastors and teachers were to continue until we all reach unity, become mature and attain the full-ness of Christ (verse 13). That determines the duration of these office gifts, but what about their purpose? Verse 12 tells us they are meant to prepare us for works of service so the Church can be built up. This is still a need in the Church today.

Ephesians 4:30 says, "And do not grieve the Holy Spirit of God, with whom you were sealed for the day of redemption." The Holy Spirit's sealing was unto the day of redemption. I believe we can grieve Him by not listening to Him, by ig-noring Him and by not exercising His "gracelets," His grace packages to us. (If I offered you a gift and you refused it, it would certainly grieve my spirit.)

Ephesians 5:18 says, "Do not get drunk on wine, which leads to debauchery. Instead, be filled with the Spirit." The word for *filled* here is in a verb tense that means "keep being filled." We note that those who were characterized as "men full of the Holy Spirit" in the New Testament were also those who were moving in healing, miracles, signs and wonders. This was especially true of Stephen and Philip, who were chosen due to being full of the Spirit.

Ephesians 6 urges us to put on the full armor of God. Verse 10 admonishes us to "be strong in the Lord and in his mighty power." Along with that, we are to "pray in the Spirit on all occasions with all kinds of prayers and requests. With this in mind, be alert and always keep on praying for all the saints" (verse 18). The way to be strong in the Lord is by putting on the whole armor of God and by praying in the Spirit. Many commentators believe this praying in the Spirit may be a reference to praying in tongues.

Philippians 1:9–11 reveals the inner working of the Spirit in our lives to make us fruitful:

> And this is my prayer: that your love may abound more and more in knowledge and depth of insight, so that you may be able to discern what is best and may be pure and blameless until the day of Christ, filled with the fruit of righteousness that comes through Jesus Christ—to the glory and praise of God.

The passage begins by saying our love opens us up to more and more "knowledge and depth of insight" (verse 9). This love is a fruit of the Holy Spirit and is always listed first because of its priority and importance. Much has been made of making the fruit a better alternative to the gifts. But both the gifts and fruit are said to be "of the Spirit" in Scripture. This "knowledge" is of Him, I believe. And this "depth of insight" is insight into His will and His ways. It is taught by the Spirit as Paul mentions in other places, and it causes us to be "able to discern what is best." It also causes us to walk in purity and be blameless. This condition is to continue "until the day of Christ"—a reference to His Second Coming (verse 10). Until that day, as verse 11 says, we are to be "filled with the fruit of righteousness that comes through Jesus Christ." This fruit is both the moral fruit of Galatians 5 and the fruit of the power of God for signs, wonders, working of miracles, healings, prophecy, words of knowledge, words of wisdom, discerning of spirits, gifts of faith, tongues and interpretation of tongues.

"Fruit of righteousness" does not refer to righteousness itself or imputed righteousness. Nor does it refer to what happened to us at salvation. Another way of seeing the fruit of righteousness and glory verse 11 talks about is to see that *glory* equals *power* and *fruit* equals both the fruit of supernatural deeds Jesus mentions in John 15 and the moral fruit Paul lists in Galatians 5:22–23. Paul also sees these fruits of righteousness through Jesus Christ bringing glory and praise to God in this passage. In John 15 Jesus is speaking not about moral fruit, but fruit that consists of supernatural deeds done by those who would be His disciples. Those who had been authorized to ask the Father in Jesus' name in prayer would be able to bear much fruit, and by doing so bring glory to the Father. The whole Upper Room Discourse in John chapters 14–16 reveals that both the Father and the Son would receive glory through acts of faith done through Jesus' followers. Both Paul and Jesus connect *fruit* to bringing glory to God—as in the fruit of supernatural works done by the disciples. Yet I believe we often read *fruit* only in light of the

Galatians 5 passage dealing with moral attributes. We also need to think of *fruit* as dealing with power gifts and works.

James 5:16 also makes the connection between Paul's "fruit of righteousness" and power: "Therefore, confess your sins to one another and pray for one another, so that you may be healed. The intense prayer of the righteous is very powerful" (HCSB, emphasis added). Though the preceding passages in James deal with moral attributes, this passage clearly is speaking not about moral attributes of righteousness, but about the power of a righteous person's prayer to effect healing. This is backed by James's immediate reference to the prophet Elijah shutting up the heavens so that it did not rain until he prayed again for rain, then it rained (see James 5:17–18). This should be the litmus test for the meaning of James 5:13–16, not James 3:17, where *fruit* obviously refers to righteous moral behavior.

Through Jesus Christ, Christians would be empowered to do works of righteousness—healing, miracles, signs and wonders—as the *fruit* Jesus spoke of in John 15:8 when He said, "This is to my Father's glory, that you bear much fruit, showing yourselves to be my disciples." Jesus and the Father would be in Christians through the Holy Spirit. Out of the greater intimacy where our love increases, so does personal revelation of God's will via the Holy Spirit. This is the main theme of John 15:1–8, and the whole of John chapters 14–16.

In summary, the "fruit of righteousness" means moral fruit *and* supernatural deeds, miracles and healings. These all come by the Spirit. How do the latter come? They come through intimacy with God—having insight and knowledge not of doctrine or theology, but of God Himself. As we learn His ways and learn how to hear His communications, these revelations are the source of our faith to produce the fruits of righteousness. It is not an *either/or*—moral fruit *or* fruits that are works of power—it is a *both/and*. As shown in James, we do not find one or the other, but both/and morality and power. Believers display *both* moral fruit and fruits of righteousness that are works of power.

In Colossians 1:9–12, we again see in Paul's prayers his deep desire for Christians to experience a personal knowledge of God and the power of God:

> For this reason, since the day we heard about you, we have not stopped praying for you and asking God to fill you with the *knowledge of his will through all spiritual wisdom and understanding.* And we pray this in order that you may live a life worthy of the Lord and may please him in every way: *bearing fruit in every good work, growing in the knowledge of God, being strengthened with all power* according to his glorious might so that you may have great endurance and patience, and joyfully giving thanks to the Father, who has qualified you to share in the inheritance of the saints in the kingdom of light [emphasis added].

Once again we see the knowledge of God's will being tied to "spiritual wisdom and understanding" (verse 9). Could this spiritual wisdom and understanding be another way of referring to the gifts of words of wisdom and words of knowledge? How do we live a life worthy of the Lord and please Him in every way? By "bearing fruit in every good work" (verse 10). How are we to bear fruit in every good work? We do this through "growing in the knowledge of God" (verse 10). We must not mistake knowledge *about* God for *knowing* God. They are completely different. I know a lot *about* President Obama, but I do not *know* him. How are we "strengthened with all power according to his glorious might" (verse 11)? Again, it is through gaining spiritual wisdom and understanding that comes from our study of the Bible *and* our experience of hearing from God through present communications from Him. As Jesus said in John 10:27, "My sheep hear My voice" (NKJV).

First Thessalonians 1:4–8 says,

> For we know, brothers loved by God, that he has chosen you, because our gospel came to you not simply with words, *but also with power, with the Holy Spirit and with deep conviction.* You know how we lived among you for your sake. You became imitators of us and of the Lord; in spite of severe suffering, you welcomed the message with the joy given by the Holy Spirit. And so you became a model to all the believers in Macedonia and Achaia. The Lord's message rang out from you not only in Macedonia and Achaia—your faith in God has become known everywhere [emphasis added].

The power referred to here has often been interpreted as the deep conviction seen in periods of great revival. But I do not agree because in the same sentence Paul lists power, the Holy Spirit and deep conviction. To make *power* the same as *deep conviction* is redundant and does not seem to do justice to the text. *Power* more likely refers to the power for healing, miracles, signs and wonders. This power that the Thessalonians experienced themselves enabled them to imitate Paul and his apostolic team and to imitate Jesus. In so doing, they were able to declare the Lord's message everywhere, not only in Macedonia and Achaia. This Gospel they declared was not just reconciliation, forgiveness and imputed righteousness, but also that the power of God was at hand because the Kingdom of God was near. Therefore, they were to exercise this power because they were seated with Christ in heavenly places and had been given all authority.

Look at 1 Thessalonians 5:16–24:

> Be joyful always; pray continually; give thanks in all circumstances, for this is God's will for you in Christ Jesus.

> Do not put out the Spirit's fire; *do not treat prophecies with contempt.* Test everything. Hold on to the good. Avoid every kind of evil.
>
> May God himself, the God of peace, sanctify you through and through. May your whole spirit, soul and body be kept blameless at the coming of our Lord Jesus Christ. The one who calls you is faithful and he will do it [emphasis added].

I believe the admonition "do not treat prophecies with contempt" implies that not all prophecies carry the same value or same anointing. Some would not be as powerful as others. The weak prophecies were the ones that could be treated with contempt. Also, the context for these verses is until the "coming of our Lord Jesus Christ."

Second Thessalonians 1:11–12 says,

> With this in mind, we constantly pray for you, that our God may count you worthy of his calling, and that *by his power he may fulfill every good purpose of yours and every act prompted by your faith.* We pray this *so that the name of our Lord Jesus may be glorified in you, and you in him,* according to the grace of our God and the Lord Jesus Christ [emphasis added].

We see once again the close connection between the name of our Lord being glorified in us and the Lord fulfilling, by His power, every good purpose of ours and every act prompted by our faith. These *purposes* and *acts* more naturally fit into the category of deeds of service and power than they do the category of moral attributes. And the *faith* referred to is still according to the grace that comes from God. That is the meaning of the word for gifts in the Bible, *charismata*— "gracelets" or "grace gifts." This faith is a gift and comes from receiving personal revelation from God. We speak because of what we believe, but our belief comes out of our relationship with Him, and our revelation from Him. We have faith sometimes as a result of seeing His faithfulness in certain areas, so frequently we now have faith for miraculous power to come without a word of knowledge or prophecy. In other situations, we have faith that comes as the gift of faith. And in still other situations, our faith is connected to the revelation that came as a result of a word of knowledge or a prophetic word. How long should we expect the duration of the application of these verses? As long as it is important that the "name of the Lord Jesus be glorified through us."

Consider Hebrews 2:4, "God also testified to it by signs, wonders and various miracles, and gifts of the Holy Spirit distributed according to his will." The *it* refers to the message of the Gospel of the Kingdom, and the gifts were part and parcel of the Kingdom. They confirmed the message, not the messengers. As long as the message needs to be given, the gifts will need to be given by God. Today, it is the power of the sign gifts that causes unbelievers to turn and believe in the message. This is especially true in non-Christian cultures, particularly among the Muslims, Hindus and Buddhists.

In his book *Christianizing the Roman Empire: A.D. 100–400* (Yale University Press, 1986), Professor Ramsay MacMullen reveals that it was the power to deliver and heal in Jesus' name that caused the adherents of other religions of the Roman Empire to forsake their former religions and come to Christ (see 4, 25). This was their main reason for conversion. They believed the message because of the powerful ministry in the authority of Jesus' name and the power of the gifts at work in His name. I have found that this is still true today. Several missionaries have told me they discovered that of all the missionaries living on the Sinai Peninsula, none have led a Muslim to the Lord unless that Muslim first sees a healing, a miracle, a dream, a vision or a revelation of Jesus.

First Peter 1:3–5 shows that God's power is to shield us until the salvation that is consummated in the last time:

> Praise be to the God and Father of our Lord Jesus Christ! In his great mercy he has given us new birth into a living hope through the resurrection of Jesus Christ from the dead, and into an inheritance that can never perish, spoil or fade—kept in heaven for you, who through faith are *shielded by God's power until the coming of the salvation that is ready to be revealed in the last time* [emphasis added].

In 1 Peter 4:7–12, Peter is anticipating the end of time coming soon. He says,

> The end of all things is near. Therefore be clear minded and self-controlled so that you can pray. . . . Each one should use whatever gift he has received to serve others, faithfully administering God's grace in its various forms. If anyone speaks, he should do it as one speaking the very words of God. If anyone serves, he should do it with the strength God provides, so that in all things God may be praised through Jesus Christ. To him be the glory and the power for ever and ever. Amen.

Peter admonishes in verse 10 that each of us should use whatever gift we have received to serve others and faithfully administer God's grace in its various forms. When I read that, it comes to mind that a gift is a form of God's grace. The various gifts reflect various forms of grace. In this light, to say that some of the gifts ended would be tantamount to saying some of God's grace ended. Nothing in the text hints that these forms of God's grace were to end before the end of time.

In 1 John 2:26–28, John refers to an anointing from God that is to remain in us:

I am writing these things to you about those who are trying to lead you astray. As for you, *the anointing you received from him remains in you*, and you do not need anyone to teach you. But as his anointing teaches you about all things and *as that anointing is real, not counterfeit*—just as it has taught you, remain in him.

And now, dear children, continue in him, *so that when he appears we may be confident and unashamed before him at his coming* [emphasis added].

This anointing can teach us about all things. It is real, not counterfeit. The context of this text is continuing in Him so we will be confident and unashamed before Him at His coming—a reference to His Second Coming. Nothing within this text or its context indicates that a time would arise when we would no longer need this anointing or when it would be taken away from us.

## Power Goes with Proclamation

So far in this chapter, I have indicated many biblical reasons to believe that God intended the gifts to continue until Jesus' Second Coming. Now let's study Scripture to see how important the dimension of *power* was to the actual preaching of the Gospel. One after another, the following verses show the centrality of power in the Church's missionary enterprise.

Both Matthew 22:29 and Mark 12:24 record Jesus' comment to some questioning Sadducees who were "in error" because they did not know "the Scriptures or the power of God." These parallel verses point out two ways of being in error—not knowing the Scriptures and not knowing the power of God.

In Luke 9:1, Jesus called the Twelve together and gave them power and authority to drive out all demons and to cure diseases. In Luke 10, the seventy-two He sent out returned with joy, saying, "Lord, even the demons submit to us in your name" (verse 17).

To that, Jesus replied, "I saw Satan fall like lightning from heaven. I have given you authority to trample on snakes and scorpions and to overcome all the power of the enemy; nothing will harm you. However, do not rejoice that the spirits submit to you, but rejoice that your names are written in heaven" (verses 18–20).

Both the Twelve and the seventy-two were authorized to heal people and cast out devils. But more importantly, they were to rejoice that their names were written in heaven. These commissions are important in our understanding of the Great Commission, which we will consider shortly.

Two verses connect power, the promise of the Father and the outpouring of the Holy Spirit. Luke 24:49 says, "I am going to send you what my Father has promised; but stay in the city until you have been clothed with power from on high." Acts 1:8 says, "But you will receive power when the Holy Spirit comes on you; and you will be my witnesses in Jerusalem, and in all Judea and Samaria, and to the ends of the earth." It has been said that there are hundreds of promises in the Bible, but there is only one "promise of the Father." The greatest promise and greatest inheritance is this promise of power. The power is made known through the energies of God, as the Orthodox would express it. Paul also speaks of the "energy" (Greek *energeia*) of God working in him in Colossians 1:29. These energies are the gifts of the Holy Spirit. The baptism with the Holy Spirit is a primary example.

Peter helps us see in Acts 3:12 that the power that works through us is not our power. We stand in a role of dependence. Peter asked the crowd who were amazed by the healing of the beggar at the Temple gate, "Men of Israel, why does this surprise you? Why do you stare at us as if by our own power or godliness we had made this man walk?" We cannot manipulate this power. Rather than us using this power, the Lord uses *us* by releasing His power through us.

Look at "much grace" in the context of Acts 4:28–33:

> "They did what your power and will had decided beforehand should happen. Now, Lord, consider their threats and enable your servants to speak your word with great boldness. Stretch out your hand to heal and perform miraculous signs and wonders through the name of your holy servant Jesus."
>
> After they prayed, the place where they were meeting was shaken. And they were all filled with the Holy Spirit and spoke the word of God boldly.
>
> All the believers were one in heart and mind. No one claimed that any of his possessions was his own, but they shared everything they had. With great power the apostles continued to testify to the resurrection of the Lord Jesus, and much grace was upon them all.

Is "much grace" to be understood as a divine enablement to work miracles and healings or as much favor? I believe in this context it is the former. This would be consistent with the prayer in verse 30 that the Lord would heal and perform miraculous signs and wonders. There is also much debate about whether the "all filled" in this passage refers to the apostles or to the Church. If referring to the Church, it then flows better with the verses immediately following it, where much grace was upon them *all*.

Acts 6:8 links God's grace and power with great wonders and miraculous signs: "Now Stephen, a man full of God's grace and power, did great wonders and miraculous signs among the people."

Acts 19:20 states, "In this way the word of the Lord spread widely and grew in power." "In this way" in other versions is translated "so." I believe it means in the manner that the revival in Ephesus was occurring (Ephesus being the place of Paul's greatest healings and extraordinary miracles), the word of the Lord continued to spread and grew in power or prevailed over the power of darkness and witchcraft, as it had in Ephesus. How did it do this? By the power of the Gospel to heal and deliver from demonic strongholds.

We have been taught to read Romans 1:16 through the reformational lens for the meaning of salvation: "I am not ashamed of the gospel, because it is the power of God for the salvation of everyone who believes: first for the Jew, then for the Gentile." This lens only sees salvation from the perspective of escaping damnation in the Day of Judgment and only sees the work of the Holy Spirit in relationship to the issue of conversion/regeneration. It does not see salvation in the larger scope of Kingdom purposes—as about forgiveness, but also about becoming a follower of Jesus equipped by grace to communicate with God, to move in God's grace-enabled power to heal the sick, and to operate with God's delegated authority to cast out demons. The Gospel brings us the *power* of God to bring salvation in its fullest sense to people—including forgiveness, healing, deliverance and the "redemption and lift" of the poor. (The phrase "redemption and lift" is a term from sociological studies into the benefits of religion. It is used to explain the fact that in just one generation, a family who comes to Christ will see a noticeable improvement in their economic status, hence "redemption and lift." This was part of Jesus' mandate in Luke 4:18.)

The power of God is the believer's source of joy, peace and hope. Romans 15:13 says, "May the God of hope fill you with all joy and peace as you trust in him, so that you may overflow with hope by the power of the Holy Spirit." See also Colossians 1:27, which refers to "Christ in you, the hope of glory," which I believe means more than hope of receiving a glorified body. I believe it means that and *more*—it also means that because Christ is in us, we have the hope of seeing the glory of God manifested through the works we do through Him by faith—that is, healing, deliverance, miracles, signs and wonders. We must be careful that our preaching does not appear to indicate that we are serving the "I Was" or "I Will Be," but that we are serving the "I AM."

Paul sees his successful missionary work as being accomplished through Christ Himself working in him. This was done not only by what Paul had spoken, preached and declared, but also by what he had done. These signs and miracles were done through the power of the Holy Spirit, as Paul said in Romans 15:17–19:

> Therefore I glory in Christ Jesus in my service to God. I will not venture to speak of anything except what Christ has accomplished through me in leading the Gentiles to obey God by what I have *said and done—by the power of signs and miracles, through the power of the Spirit*. So from Jerusalem all the way around to Illyricum, *I have fully proclaimed the gospel of Christ* [emphasis added].

It was not just the preaching or the healing and miracles that accomplished the work of the Gospel—it was the combination of the two. Can we believe we have *fully* proclaimed the Gospel of Christ when signs and miracles are not accompanying the preaching?

In 1 Corinthians 2:2–5, Paul said,

> For I resolved to know nothing while I was with you except Jesus Christ and him crucified. I came to you in weakness

and fear, and with much trembling. My message and my preaching were not with wise and persuasive words, but with a demonstration of the Spirit's power, so that your faith might not rest on men's wisdom, but on God's power.

This famous passage indicates the importance of preaching with a demonstration of the Spirit's power. The new believers at Corinth were the actual evidence of the Spirit's power. But Paul's modus operandi was to communicate the message of the cross, which included Jesus' resurrection and His pouring out of the Holy Spirit as a sign that the Kingdom of God had begun, a Kingdom that was already present, though not yet complete. The healings and miracles were signs that would point to the truth of the general resurrection, when those who were alive at the time would be totally healed and given a glorified body, just as those who had already gone to be with the Lord.

## For the Apostles or for All?

Now we have established scripturally that first, the gifts of the Spirit (especially healing and miracles in our study) were to continue until Jesus returned because their purpose was to be part of the expression of the Gospel. Second, we have established scripturally that they were vitally important to the actual preaching of the Gospel. Third, I now want to explore scripturally whether only the apostles had the gifts of healing and miracles or whether non-apostles also experienced and ministered through these gifts.

I believe Scripture shows that the power was for *all*. Ananias was not listed as an apostle, an evangelist or a deacon. He is referred to only as a *disciple*, the New Testament's most common word for a Christian. Yet look at Ananias in Acts 9:17: "Then Ananias went to the house and entered it.

Placing his hands on Saul, he said, 'Brother Saul, the Lord—Jesus, who appeared to you on the road as you were coming here—has sent me so that you may see again and be filled with the Holy Spirit.'"

Those who were scattered in Acts 11:19–21 were not apostles. The apostles stayed in Jerusalem:

> Now those who had been scattered by the persecution in connection with Stephen traveled as far as Phoenicia, Cyprus and Antioch, telling the message only to Jews. Some of them, however, men from Cyprus and Cyrene, went to Antioch and began to speak to Greeks also, telling them the good news about the Lord Jesus. The Lord's hand was with them, and a great number of people believed and turned to the Lord.

These who were scattered were not called evangelists or deacons either. They were the rank and file, the "little ole me's" of the Church. And the phrase "the Lord's hand was with them" in verse 21 means the power of God was present (see also Exodus 9:3; Acts 13:11). In this case, the power of God was demonstrated by accompanying the message with signs following.

Note that back in Mark 16:20, the signs are not following the *apostles*, but following the *preaching* of the word. (Note also that the fact that this portion of Mark is not in the oldest extant manuscripts does not mean it is not inspired—it was the Church that established the Canon of Scripture, and this ending was deemed inspired. Either the Church knew the ending was in older manuscripts no longer in existence, or the saying was so true to the apostolic message that it was deemed inspired and authoritative.)

In John 14:12, Jesus states, "I tell you the truth, anyone who has faith in me will do what I have been doing. He will do even greater things than these, because I am going to the

Father." *Anyone* here actually means *anyone* and is not limited to the apostles. Jesus does not say "anyone who believes in Me for the next two hundred years" (or until the Bible is canonized) will do great things; He simply says *anyone*. The NKJV translation of this verse says, "Most assuredly, I say to you, he who believes in Me, the works that I do he will also do; and greater works than these will he do, because I go to My Father" (see also the NRSV's similar translation). Many New Testament scholars have pointed out that the Greek term *erga* used in John 14:12 to mean "works" denotes *miraculous works*. So Jesus is saying that anyone who has faith in Him will do the *same miraculous works that He did*. (I want to thank Dr. Gary Greig for providing me with this insight.)

According to Matthew 28:18–20, baptized believers were to be taught to obey everything Jesus commanded:

> Then Jesus came to them and said, "All authority in heaven and on earth has been given to me. Therefore go and make disciples of all nations, baptizing them in the name of the Father and of the Son and of the Holy Spirit, and teaching them to obey everything I have commanded you. And surely I am with you always, to the very end of the age."

The persons baptized as a result of Jesus' instructions were not apostles, but those who were yet to become disciples. And those new disciples were to obey everything Jesus commanded the apostles to do—the number one thing being to heal and deliver.

To obey is to do as you are told. It has also been translated "to observe" in this passage, but I feel such a translation misses the mark of Jesus' intent. The Greek verb *terein* clearly means "to obey commands" in Matthew 28:20, but it means the same elsewhere as well (see Matthew 19:17; 23:3). In New Testament times, a disciple did not simply learn what the master taught;

he also followed the lifestyle of the master/mentor/teacher. Dr. Jon Ruthven's book dealing with discipleship and training makes this fact clear; for more from him on this, see *What Is Wrong With Protestant Theology?* (Word & Spirit Press, 2011).

Discipleship is more than observing—watching, viewing, scrutinizing, monitoring, studying, examining, surveying—it is becoming like the teacher by doing what one is told. This is the root of our theological education problem. We have mistaken *studying the Master* for *becoming like Him*. We have mistaken *observing* for *doing*. We have replaced the Jewish understanding of discipleship with a Greek understanding. The New Testament was written by Jews, with a Jewish understanding of discipleship, not with a Greek understanding.

In Mark 16:15–20, Jesus teaches us that signs follow those who believe (not just the apostles). Notice that He does not attach an expiration date to this commission. Several of the sign gifts are specifically listed in this passage:

> He said to them, "Go into all the world and preach the good news to all creation. Whoever believes and is baptized will be saved, but whoever does not believe will be condemned. And these signs will accompany those who believe: In my name they will drive out demons; they will speak in new tongues; they will pick up snakes with their hands; and when they drink deadly poison, it will not hurt them at all; they will place their hands on sick people, and they will get well."
>
> After the Lord Jesus had spoken to them, he was taken up into heaven and he sat at the right hand of God. Then the disciples went out and preached everywhere, and the Lord worked with them and confirmed his word by the signs that accompanied it.

It is of huge import that verse 20 teaches that the signs accompanied "it," meaning the Gospel, not "them," which would have meant the apostles.

Dr. Wayne Grudem contributed a chapter titled "Should Christians Expect Miracles Today?" to the book *The Kingdom and the Power: Are Healing and the Spiritual Gifts Used by Jesus and the Early Church Meant for the Church Today?* (Regal, 1993). In his chapter, Dr. Grudem answers the assertion that miracles were primarily done by the apostles (60–61):

> The unusual concentration of miracles in the ministries of the apostles does not prove that *no miracles* were performed by others. As we have clearly seen, "working of miracles" (1 Cor. 12:10 and other miraculous gifts; 1 Cor. 12:4–11 mentions several) were part of the ordinary function of the Corinthian church, and Paul knows that God "works miracles" in the churches of Galatia as well (Gal. 3:5).
>
> In the larger context of the New Testament, it is clear that miracles were worked by others who were not apostles, such as Stephen (Acts 6:8), Philip (Acts 8:6–7), Ananias (Acts 9:17–18; 22:13), Christians in the several churches in Galatia (Gal. 3:5) and those with gifts of "miracles" in the Body of Christ generally (1 Cor. 12:10, 28). Miracles as such cannot then be regarded as exclusively signs of an apostle. "Workers of miracles" and "healers" are actually *distinguished* from "apostles" in 1 Cor. 12:28; "And God has appointed in the church first apostles, second prophets, third teachers, then workers of miracles, then healers."

Based on 2 Corinthians 12:12, some have argued that miracles were exclusively the signs of an apostle: "The things that mark an apostle—signs, wonders and miracles—were done among you with great perseverance." But this is not what the Greek language emphasizes. The signs of an apostle that Paul mentions include many things, among them miracles and healing, but those were not done exclusively by apostles, as our study already has pointed out.

Dr. Grudem also deals with the argument that only the apostles and those closely associated with them, or those on whom the apostles laid their hands, could work miracles. He demonstrates the insufficiency of such an argument by pointing out that in the New Testament, only the apostles or those closely associated with them did missionary work and planted churches. By this line of reasoning, then, not only would healing and miracles be considered strictly the domain of the apostolic and therefore not for today, but so would missions and church planting. (See *The Kingdom and the Power*, 61.)

Our study of the Scriptures conclusively indicates that the function or purpose of healings and miracles was to be part of the expression of the Gospel. The sign gifts were to continue until Jesus' Second Coming because they were part of the Good News about the inbreak of the Kingdom. They are the energies of God that make the power of God, as well as the presence of God, tangible today. They are the means by which the strong man's house is plundered (see Matthew 12:29). They are part of the Gospel and should accompany it. They confirm the Gospel. There is a difference between confirming the Gospel and confirming doctrines and Scripture.

We also have seen that the aspect of power as part of the preaching of the Gospel was central to the New Testament perspective. We saw this especially in Matthew 13's parables of Jesus regarding the Kingdom and in Matthew 28's Great Commission, in light of the other commissions given to the Twelve and the seventy-two. New Testament scholar Dr. Craig Keener believes those are clearly meant by the gospel writers as paradigms for the discipleship of others who would become Christians. For more from him on this, see his book *Gift & Giver: The Holy Spirit for Today* (Baker Academic, 2001). We also saw it in the writings of Paul and in Hebrews 2:4.

We have seen that the gifts of healing and working of miracles were not exclusively the domain of the apostles or those on whom the apostles laid hands. They occurred at the hands of non-apostles and their delegates as well. Some examples are Philip, Stephen, Ananias (who prayed for Paul to be healed and filled with the Spirit) and the unnamed disciples mentioned in Act 11:21: "The Lord's hand was with them, and a great number of people believed and turned to the Lord." The phrase "The Lord's hand was with them" refers to the miraculous power of God.

## Real-Life Benefits of the Gifts

A solid exegesis of the Bible and sound theological arguments have been important in helping us clarify our thinking about these positions. However, I want to end this chapter as I began it, with a real-life story about the beneficial nature of the gifts. Again, these gifts are not limited to evidential purposes—their primary purpose is to make the mercy, love and power of God tangible to us today. They have certainly done that for me. During the last few years, I had a scary experience with my back. One time, I was seated on the floor at home as I entertained some of my pastoral advisors for the network of churches and itinerate ministries I oversee. We were having a conference the next day. When I tried to get up, I experienced the worst pain of my life. The only thing that compared to it was the spinal injury from the car wreck I was in at eighteen.

I could not put my foot on the floor or put any pressure on it, nor could I straighten it out without excruciating pain. I ended up at the doctor's office and found out there was neurological damage in my spine. I was given Percocet, a powerful painkiller, along with a drug to reduce the swelling in my nerves and prescription-strength Ibuprofen (800 milligrams). Even taking all those, the pain was terrible. I could not move an eighth of an inch off my bed without excruciating pain.

I went to physical therapy six days a week for ninety days. I was unable to walk without crutches, could not sit in a chair without exacerbating the problem and was reduced to lying on a mat or lying in bed. Eventually I was given two epidurals. The physical therapist told me that if those did not help, I would probably need back surgery. They did not help. I had four herniated discs and two pinched nerves, along with two forms of arthritis in my spine.

I found out that the cause of my problem was my many long international airplane trips. My condition was called "traveler's back." The lower lumbar lordosis (curve of the spine) had been lost, and my lumbar was flat instead of curved. This condition allowed for the discs to slip easily. I was told the best thing for me was to never get on another airplane. I was in pain 24/7. Even in my sleep, I moaned in pain. Later, a neurosurgeon I met told me one of my pinched nerves was the most painful nerve in the body to pinch. That was no surprise to me.

Whether or not healing and the gifts of the Spirit continued on today was more than an academic question to me. I needed healing or needed surgery. Many friends known for their strong healing gifts prayed for me, but I was not healed through their prayers. Instead, I was healed through two people not noted for healing.

The first breakthrough came when my oldest son, Josh, called me from Japan on Skype and prayed an amazing prayer. What authority he prayed with—I could not believe this was coming from my 28-year-old son. When he was done, my pain was gone. Not all the pain; it still hurt to put weight on my foot. I still could not go up steps normally or walk without crutches. But before his prayer, I was in pain 24/7. After his prayer, I was in pain only if I put weight on my leg.

I continued in this improved condition for quite some time. Then one morning I woke up and reached for my crutches, and when my foot touched the floor, I noticed it did not cause pain. I stood up without the crutches—no pain! I went to our staircase and went up the steps normally. I was amazed. I had gone to bed with the usual pain when I put pressure on my leg, but woke up without it.

Later that day, I received an amazing email. An oil-and-gas businessman whom I knew, who had been with me in Brazil and India, had been at a church meeting. During the service, he went into an open vision. He saw me and saw my spine. In the vision, Jesus told him what was wrong with my spine and how to pray for it, including acting out pushing the disc material that had squirted out of the disc back in. He was so shocked by the experience that he sent me an email to see how I was doing.

I called him when I received his email, and we talked. I was excited that my pain was gone—but even more excited when I found out how the healing had happened. The fact that God had given this vision to my friend Ray was such a blessing to me.

All I know is that I am glad that the gifts of healing and miracles are still available for the Church today. My family and I have been real-life beneficiaries of them more than once. In the case of my traveler's back, one of the most painful conditions I have ever experienced, I am glad someone had a visual word of knowledge for me and prayed the prayer of faith, and I was healed.

# 4

## UNBELIEVING BELIEVERS AND BELIEVING UNBELIEVERS

### *Randy*

When I was in seminary, one course I took on the book of Acts required a term paper. The professor gave us about fifty subjects to choose from, but healing was not among them. Because I was very interested in healing, I wanted to write on the subject. I thought it was consistent with the word I had received my first day of college: "The Holy Spirit will be the issue of your lifetime." So I asked, "Could I write on healing? It's in the book of Acts."

The professor answered, "You may, but you cannot use anecdotal stories, you must do good research."

I began my research in what was either the largest or second-largest theological library in the world at the time—only to be surprised by how few books it contained on healing. Using what I did find, I wrote the paper and received an A on it, along with numerous comments from the professor. He told me he had never written so much on a student's paper before and that it was a compliment to the paper's quality. However, his comments included several warnings. He warned me not to be too harsh on those who did not believe in healing for today. He said I had written as if healing were central to the Gospel, which he did not believe. To him healing was a peripheral issue, not a central issue.

I told him I disagreed, and today I am even more committed than I was back then to the position that healing is central to the Gospel. I recently found that term paper, which I kept for over thirty years. Here is the final paragraph:

> The miraculous element in Christianity and the fact that God can act in this world of ours is essential to the vitality of Christianity. Without this aspect, prayer becomes meaning-less and one should study the social sciences rather than the Bible, and Theology should be replaced with Anthropology. Preaching that is void of the above concepts is one reason for the phenomenal growth of the Charismatic Movement. Just as Jeremiah criticized the Israelites for creating with their hands gods who were helpless, modern man has created a "god" who is helpless to act in this world. A god this writer refuses to worship.

That final paragraph hooked the professor. Initially he overreacted in his comments, then he wrote that he over-reacted and that he did not find me dogmatic in class. He warned me, though, that if I believed in healing this strongly and taught on it in the future, I would have problems in Baptist churches. This proved true. But "The Times They Are A-Changin'," as Bob Dylan sang in his song of that title. The answer to the cry in people's hearts is "Blowin' in the Wind," as another of his song titles suggests. In New

Testament Greek and Hebrew, the words for *wind* and *spirit* are the same. The changes we have seen are the result of the moving of the Holy Spirit.

I experienced rejection from some Baptists in 1984 for my belief in healing and the gifts. But I have also preached in the largest Baptist church in South Africa, the largest Baptist church in Brazil and the oldest and second-largest Baptist church in Argentina. I have seen healings in all those churches, and they are all open to the gifts of the Spirit. The times are indeed changing. The Holy Spirit is like the wind and brings with Him the answer to our human needs.

## Winds of Change

I have seen the winds of change evident in many places. Let me tell you the story of one "traditional" Baptist church in Mauve, Brazil. When I first visited, it was a small church of about 300 located on the wrong side of the tracks, down a dirt road in a poor area. The pastor was hungry for God's touch and wanted to experience His presence in the services. We were there only a few days, yet so many healings happened that it was amazing. Almost every member of his staff was healed of something. One man was healed of a terrible case of psoriasis, a genetic disease without a cure. Nine years later, he told me it had never come back. God can change our DNA!

One woman with several illnesses had twisted legs. One leg turned out almost 180 degrees from her body. She was totally healed of everything, and her leg rotated back to normal. People with illnesses of all kinds could not get into the sanctuary because it was full. Many of them were healed in the hallways or outside as they stood in the yard and listened through the windows.

What was the fruit for this Baptist church? Three years later, we returned to find that it was no longer on the wrong side of the tracks. It had moved to one of the city's main streets and had grown to three thousand. We held another powerful healing meeting there, then we did not return again for six years. We came back a third time to find a congregation of nine thousand attending the main church and five thousand more attending four satellite churches around the city. This time we had the greatest meeting of all. The atmosphere became electric with the power of God. Hundreds were healed—the blind, the deaf, the paralyzed from a stroke who could not talk or walk. Cancerous tumors disappeared. Cartilage that had been destroyed for twenty years was recreated. A polio case was healed. People in terrible pain from metal in their bodies were healed. One man had had numerous screws and rods put in his back two months before the meeting and could not stand the pain. Now he was bending over and touching his toes, bending his back backward and jumping up and down. All these testimonies resulted from just one amazing night—and we were in Brazil two whole weeks. Every night we saw hundreds of healings.

The next year we returned again. By then, the pastor had sent out groups to start 23 other churches in the city. This time, on the second night 60 people were healed in the pre-service prayer time one hour before service. During this hour we prayed only for those with visual or hearing problems, those who could not walk normally or needed an aid to walk and those who had a terminal illness. Again the blind, deaf and crippled were healed. One little boy with a clubfoot just wanted to run. After prayer, his foot rotated and he did run! Two people with aneurisms were healed; one of them had gone blind and had not been able to see in 8 months. The other had lost 90 percent of his hearing and was paralyzed on his left side. Both my team and the people of the church were ecstatic. Before the night was over, several hundred more people were healed through words of knowledge and the laying on of hands. Our ministry team totaled nearly 75 and came from several countries.

The pastor told me that other Baptist pastors were asking why his church was growing so much while theirs were not. He would reply, "You know those things you don't like? They are the reason."

Susan Starr, one of the women who had prayed for the little boy with the clubfoot, had also seen every other person she prayed for healed. Susan is a member of a cessationist church— someone whose doctrinal associations discount healing and miracles. But in practice and experience, by all means Susan believes! Her very presence challenges her church's doctrinal position because she was once in hospice, close to death. Preparing to die, she had even given away her winter clothes. She was in severe pain, her autonomic nervous system did not work, three feet of her colon was removed, and she would pass out after standing more than two minutes. Yet Susan was healed. She came on our trip to Brazil specifically so she would have an opportunity to pray for other people, and she did! During her two-week trip, she prayed for many serious conditions including a tumor behind one young man's eyes. It had caused severe headaches, and he could not even walk fast without passing out. He was healed, his headaches left and he could not only walk fast—he could run! (I believe this indicated that the tumor was disappearing.) If you tried to convince Susan that healing is not for today, you probably would not get very far.

## What Are Unbelieving Believers?

Amazing stories like Susan's cause me to ask why we have so many unbelieving believers. I want to suggest multiple reasons

91

for this situation, but first let's consider what the question means. By *believers* I mean people who attend church on a regular basis, who have committed themselves as followers of Jesus Christ and who have been regenerated by the Holy Spirit. I use the word *unbelieving* in the sense of not believing that certain gifts of the Holy Spirit are for the Church today. Those gifts, called the sign gifts by cessationists, would be healing, the working of miracles, tongues, the interpretation of tongues, and prophecy. Technically, the doctrinal system of cessationism views all of these gifts as no longer operational. However, for my purposes here, I will address mainly unbelief in healing and miracles.

What about the *believing unbelievers* I have mentioned? By *unbelievers* I mean those who have not been regenerated by the Holy Spirit and have not committed their lives to following Jesus Christ. They have not become part of a local church, yet many of these unbelievers are *believing* in the sense that they are completely open to the power of God and the gifts of healing in operation today. Many experience healings outside the walls of a church.

For example, the bakery workers I talked about in chapter 1 were what I call believing unbelievers. Remember that I prayed for them at the Kroger stores during my "great experiment" of praying for people outside the Church? Most did not claim to be committed believers in any way—yet time after time, they were open to allowing me to pray. And time after time, they were healed. I related some of those instances in chapter 1, so I will not talk too much more about them here.

Contrast these believing unbelievers, however, with the unbelieving believers present in large numbers in church who are skeptical of God's power for healing and miracles. These believers are closed to experiencing the operation of the gifts today. Why is it that so many Christians become "unbelieving believers" when it comes to the gifts? I want to note three primary contributing causes: sociological factors, theological factors and church factors. Sociological factors are those that in some way impact the Church's purity and power or affect the Church's focus on this world or the next. When the Church's focus is more on the next world (by which I mean a focus on the Second Coming of Christ), less emphasis is put on healing in this world.

Society's prevailing philosophy is also a factor. A case in point is the modernistic worldview—a closed world in which God does not intervene in the affairs of men, nor does He violate His laws of nature. Until the last quarter century, our educational systems primarily taught modernism. Deism is a religious view based on the sociological factor of modernism. Postmodernism, on the other hand, is much more open to the supernatural and to truth coming through "experience," whereas modernism emphasized truth coming through reason.

By theological factors I mean a theology based on the closed world system of modernism—in other words, liberalism. Another such factor would also be the theological construct of cessationism.

By church factors I refer to denominational confessions and practices that deny the continuation of the gifts and that censure those who practice the gifts or even believe in them. These factors often result in people having to resign their positions or be fired if they open themselves up to operating in the gifts of the Spirit.

Individually and together, these societal, theological and church factors contribute to the formation of "unbelieving believers" by negatively impacting people's faith for healings and miracles. Let's briefly consider these factors one at a time and look at how they affect the attitude of believers toward these gifts.

## Sociological Factors

Over the centuries, numerous sociological factors have contributed to the Church's diminishing experience of healing and miracles. The first involved the Roman Emperor Constantine's conversion to Christianity and the Edict of Milan in 313 A.D. This edict made Christianity a legal religion in the Roman Empire. Previously, persecution had kept Christianity pure. Up until that time, there were few hypocrites or nominal Christians. With the legalizing of Christianity, however, persecution ended and the Church began to include many nominal members. These members bore the name *Christian*—but not always due to a genuine conversion.

The second sociological factor was the adoption of Christianity as the official religion of the Roman Empire in 380 A.D. This caused a flood of nominal members to join the Church, which consequently was worse off than before because now many of its members were not truly converted to Christ.

Third, the fall of the Roman Empire in 476 A.D. and the terrible living conditions of the Dark Ages between 400 and 1400 A.D. caused people to focus on the next life rather than looking for healing in this life. People were anxious to escape their difficult lives on earth and move on to the next place—counting on it to be a far better place (a normal human response to terrible living conditions).

The fourth sociological factor was the scientific rationalism of the late seventeenth and eighteenth centuries. Its reliance on reason as the basis for religious truth resulted in a denial of miracles and healings, which caused many to lose faith in healing.

Fifth, the advancement of medical science was accompanied by a loss of belief in the human soul. The traditional view of the soul was rejected, and human beings were reduced to being the by-product of chemical impulses in a bodily form. Humankind has been dehumanized by the humanist movement, and the unity of body, soul and spirit has been denied. As a result, modern medicine treats the patient's symptoms with medicine rather than treating the underlying causes of sickness. This is beginning to change, however, with the field of psychosomatic medicine, which is rediscovering and affirming—though often unaware—the biblical view of a person as a whole in which if one part becomes ill, it can affect the other two. More and more, Christians are also discovering the spiritual aspects of disease and pointing to the soul as the seat of the will and emotions. It has become clearer, therefore, that when the principles of Scripture are not followed, the soul becomes sick—resulting in unforgiveness, bitterness, cynicism and judgmentalism.

## Theological Factors: Roman Catholic Church

From a theological perspective, certain factors within the Roman Catholic and Protestant churches contributed to the demise of faith in healing. In the Roman Catholic Church, the first factor involved Augustine's move from the warfare worldview to the blueprint worldview. Augustine became a Christian in 387 A.D. and died in 430. One of the strongest leaders of the Western Church, he profoundly impacted its theology. His writings were most influential in the development of Western Christianity. Prior to Augustine and for a few hundred years after him, the predominant understanding of life was the warfare worldview—that forces of evil were at war against Christ and His Church. This warfare caused the sicknesses and demonic bondages people experienced. Within this worldview, believers were to fight against sickness, disease and demonic oppression through the power of the Holy Spirit.

However, Augustine's writings eventually moved the Church to a blueprint worldview—an understanding that everything in life happens due to the predetermined will of God. This caused a shift in the thinking of the Church regarding healing. Now, instead of believing that sickness was brought on by the devil (who ought to be resisted), people believed that God brought on sickness for a person's spiritual sanctification. Therefore, to pray against an illness could be viewed as resisting God. Instead of praying for healing, believers began to pray for discernment about why God might have brought sickness or disease into someone's life.

A second factor in the Roman Catholic Church arose from Jerome's mistranslation of James 5:14–15. Properly translated, those verses read, "Is any one of you sick? He should call the elders of the church to pray over him and anoint him with oil in the name of the Lord. And the prayer offered in faith will make the sick person well; the Lord will raise him up. If he has sinned, he will be forgiven." The phrase "make the sick person well" in this translation (NIV) comes from the Greek word for *heal*. But Jerome translated the word as *save* instead. This eventually led to changing the Anointing of the Sick, which was *not* reserved for the dying, to Last Rights or Extreme Unction, a Roman Catholic set of sacraments usually given to a dying person not expected to recover.

A third theological factor was Thomas Aquinas's synthesis of Christian theology and Aristotelian philosophy in his *Summa Theologica*. This attempt to present the Gospel to the Arab world, which had changed from a society based upon Platonic philosophy to a society based upon Aristotelian philosophy, would have dramatic effects on the Church. The Church would now emphasize reason more than revelation and value the material more than the spiritual.

96

Notably, at the end of his life Aquinas again changed his views as the result of an experience he had on December 6, 1273. After that experience he wrote, *"I can write no more. All I have written seems so much straw compared with what I have seen and what has been revealed to me."* Three months later he died on a mission trip for the Pope. Others had to finish his famous *Summa Theologica*, and we do not know how his experience would have changed his theology, had he lived long enough to process it into his theology.

Fourth, the Roman Church's understanding of the gifts of the Spirit moved from an emphasis on the supernatural aspects to an understanding of the gifts based on much more natural aspects. For example, Pope Gregory the Great, whose papacy ran from 590–604, created a list of the gifts of the Spirit that consisted of wisdom, science, understanding, counsel, fortitude, piety and fear. The gifts of healing and the working of miracles were not mentioned in his list. Neither were words of knowledge, words of wisdom or prophecy.

A fifth factor was that healings, miracles and the dead being raised came to be used as evidence of true doctrine or the deity of Christ. This evidential function should be seen as a secondary purpose of the gifts, not their primary purpose. The primary purpose of healings and miracles is the demonstration of the Gospel and the goodness of God.

Sixth was that the Roman Church's theology did not distinguish the context of Jesus' references to suffering, or later Paul's references. Mistakenly, suffering in sickness was seen as carrying our cross and glorifying Jesus in our suffering—whereas instead suffering should have been seen as persecution for the Gospel.

These factors and their resultant shifts in the thinking of the Roman Catholic Church would also affect the Protestant church, which never challenged most of them. But other factors would affect the Protestant church without having as great an effect on the Roman Church. We will look at those factors next.

## Theological Factors: Protestant Church

Theologically speaking, the American and European Protestant churches have been bastions of skeptical unbelief toward healing and miracles happening today. That skepticism was taught to their members. My own experiences in college and seminary have caused me to see such institutions as centers for skepticism rather than as centers to strengthen faith. At least, that has been my personal experience, and it is also how we have arrived at the dilemma of having "unbelieving believers" and "believing unbelievers." Let's look at some of the teachings that have resulted in such rampant skepticism.

### Liberalism and Cessationism

As I have already stated, I graduated from Oakland City College and The Southern Baptist Theological Seminary. My college professors in religious studies at the time were quite liberal, and the ones who were not liberal were cessationist, as were my seminary professors.

Briefly, let me explain what liberal theologians and cessationists believe. A liberal theologian does not believe in anything supernatural in the Bible, nor would a liberal believe that anything supernatural would happen today. A cessationist is on the opposite end of the theological spectrum. Usually very conservative, a cessationist believes the Bible records historical events that were certainly supernatural. But cessationists believe these events—miracles, healings, signs and wonders—ended either with the death of the last apostle or with the canonization of the Bible. They do believe God *could* work miracles today as sovereign answers to prayer. However, such answers are not seen as the norm, but rather as quite rare.

For cessationists, the gifts of healing and the working of miracles no longer exist in the sense of someone having these gifts. Their argument is based on their belief that healings and miracles were given to prove correct doctrine and to vindicate the apostles' ministry as writers of Scripture. If healings and miracles could still happen, then the canon of Scripture would not be closed and new doctrines could be given. This is the basis of cessationism.

The problem with this position is that miracles were not meant primarily as evidence of correct doctrine. Instead they were part of the Gospel, the good news that the Kingdom of God was at hand, that in Jesus' ministry the Kingdom had been inaugurated and would continue until it was consummated in His Second Coming. The cessationist position therefore violates the biblical doctrine of the Kingdom of God and the doctrine of the Holy Spirit's continued role beyond salvation. And as we saw in chapter 3, where we looked at the scriptural foundation for healing, this position contradicts the many Scriptures that teach that the gifts are to continue until Jesus' return.

When it comes to practical pastoral ministry regarding healing, the liberal and the cessationist make strange bedfellows. They both end up *not expecting* healing to occur, and they do not equip their parishioners to pray for the sick or do deliverance. Yet these are the two primary theological systems Protestant church pastors have been trained in. Liberalism has been prominent for about three hundred years now, and cessationism for five hundred. Neither system would believe in the possibility that people have the gift to heal or work miracles today. They would not teach their people to have faith for healing. Rather, they would teach them to deny present-day miracles or healings as impossible or fraudulent. It is little wonder, then, that believers within these systems develop into "unbelieving believers."

## Dispensationalism

Dispensationalism is another "ism" that has had a negative impact on the Church's faith in healing and miracles. Based on a "revelation" to fifteen-year-old Margaret MacDonald, who received it in 1830 in a vision, it is the source of the pre-Tribulation understanding of Jesus' Second Coming. Instead of a restoration of the offices and gifts active in the early Church, it taught that the Church at the end of time, just before Jesus returned, would be lukewarm and weak. It also taught that prior to the return of Jesus, lying signs and wonders would occur to lead people away from the faith.

This pre-Tribulation view was never heard of before 1830. John Darby, a leader in the Plymouth Brethren, was not only a cessationist, but also held the view that the end-time Church would be weak. Darby's views were later popularized in the notes of C. I. Scoffield in his study Bible.

This dispensationalist view is ultrapessimistic, leaving no place for an end-time victorious Church or revival. Ironically, many Pentecostals would adopt dispensationalism's end-time understanding of the Second Coming of Jesus, though they would reject its cessationist understanding of the gifts of the Holy Spirit.

## Neoorthodoxy

Neoorthodoxy is a twentieth-century development in Protestant theology. Karl Barth and Emil Brunner were its primary originators. Barth was a Reformed pastor, and in the Reformed tradition, was also a cessationist. Neoorthodoxy

100

embraced some of liberalism's antisupernatural presuppositions, but was more conservative in its conclusions. This school of theology, popular among seminaries during the twentieth century, was taught to thousands of seminarians. It was a system that did not allow—let alone expect—healings and miracles.

## New Liberalism

I have already dealt with liberalism above, but this newer kind of liberalism is even more radical than the older form, which tried to explain the supernatural by offering naturalistic causes. New liberalism more radically rejects the supernatural—in fact, its whole presupposition is a strong antisupernaturalism. Instead of trying to explain a "miracle" through naturalistic means, the event in question was not considered a real occurrence at all, but rather a story made up to teach a theological truth—a myth. But *myth* here does not mean the story was not teaching a truth; rather it meant the historical event simply never occurred. Hence there was no need to supply a naturalistic interpretation for it. The term developed for this by Rudolph Bultmann was *demythologizing* the Scripture.

This form of liberalism was characterized, then, by the demythologizing of Rudolph Bultmann and Paul Tillich. It maintained that there was no need to believe that the supernatural events of Scripture were historical. Christian faith was not to be based on whether or not events actually took place, but rather in the *theology* of the so-called myths or legends in Scripture. For clarity's sake, let me again state that here *myth* does not mean something false. Rather, *myth* actually means a story that carries in it the deep truths of the Christian faith. It was not considered necessary for a story to have actually taken place in history to make its point. Real

101

truth was to be found in the theology communicated within "mythological" stories in the New Testament.

## Fundamentalism

Fundamentalism was a reaction to the liberalism of the nineteenth and twentieth centuries. It was largely popularized by the writings of the Princeton theologian B. B. Warfield. He also wrote a book against the continuance of miracles today, *Counterfeit Miracles*, first published in 1918. A Presbyterian and a Reformed theologian, Warfield believed strongly in the cessationist view of spiritual gifts.

In the 1920s the American church experienced the modernist-fundamentalist controversy. The fundamentalists, who believed that the Bible was true historically and that supernatural events took place through the apostles until the apostles died, rose up to try to regain control of the teaching institutions of the American church. They failed, and most of the American seminaries, divinity schools and Christian colleges came under the control of the liberal viewpoint. This meant that most of the denominationally trained ministers were trained in skeptical unbelief and rejection of the supernatural—not just applicable to their present day, but also to the Bible. They would not believe the gifts of healing or working of miracles were for today.

The cessationist-fundamentalist segment responded by starting new schools. Remember, both they and the liberals believed the gifts of healing and working of miracles would not happen in the present day. More accurately, the fundamentalists believed that these gifts were no longer in existence. As stated earlier, they believed a healing could occur, but *not* due to the gifts of healing. It would be due to God sovereignly responding to intercessory prayer on behalf of the sick person, and these answers were not seen as normative, but as rare.

## Roman Catholic Church Factors

We have looked at a number of societal and theological/hermeneutical factors that led to the creation of unbelieving believers, but there is also another group of important factors to consider: the Church factors. Both the Roman Catholic and Protestant churches made decisions that negatively impacted believers' faith for healing and miracles.

Three factors within Roman Catholicism contributed to the demise of belief in healing and miracles. First, the Middle Age's period of moral corruption and its failure to correct it caused a decrease in healing. Along with the lukewarmness that settled in the Church and the consequent lack of purity, there came a corresponding lack of power.

A second factor was the gradual progression toward relegating healings and miracles to the Catholic "saints" (both before and after their deaths) and accusing common people who moved in these gifts of being involved in witchcraft. It was believed that exceptional holiness, including consecration to God as part of a religious order or the priesthood, was necessary for a person to display gifts of healing and miracles. This caused the laity to feel they were not good enough or holy enough to be used for healing. (Besides, it was dangerous! Lay persons actually were tortured or burned for practicing such gifts without having attained the supposed level of holiness.)

A third factor occurred after 1967, when the prayers of Pope John XXIII were answered for a new Pentecost in the Roman Catholic Church. This was a positive thing, but how the Catholic Church accommodated the visitation of the Spirit would ultimately have a negative impact on a belief in the gifts, in my opinion. The Catholic Church accommodated charismatic priests and people by allowing charismatic small groups and fellowships within the local parishes, but it did not allow its liturgies to become charismatic in expression. This stance isolated the charismatic dimension of the Spirit from the main liturgical services of the Catholic Church.

## Protestant Church Factors

The Protestant church contributed its own set of factors that hindered healing and miracles. Eight factors within Protestantism led to the demise of faith for the operation of these gifts. In chronological order, the first factor was the restriction of Johann Blumhardt's ministry in Germany. Blumhardt, who lived from 1805–1880, was one of the first people within Protestantism to begin praying for the sick with effectiveness. He had a powerful healing ministry—so powerful that the Lutheran denomination asked him not to pray for the sick because it was causing jealousy and problems because people kept coming from outside his parish to receive prayer. Healings and a revival broke out after he cast a demon out of a young woman. It took a two-year battle for her freedom, but the demon was finally overcome. It left screaming "Jesus is victor" and did not come back. This incident, told in Freidrich Zuendel's *The Awakening* (Plough Publishing, 2000), occurred in 1842. Blumhardt never took credit for deliverances or healings. Instead, he liked to say that there were many things he did not know, but the one thing he did know was that Jesus is victor. Because of denominational pressure not to pray for the sick as part of his parish ministry, he resigned and began a healing center in 1853.

The second factor was the defrocking (taking away the ordination) of the London Presbyterian pastor Edward Irving because he believed in the restoration of the gifts and offices of the early Church to the Church of his day. This sent a message to other pastors who might be interested in the renewal of the Spirit that it would probably cost them their church and their ordination. Irving was one of the very first Protestants to believe and preach that the gifts of the Holy Spirit were to be restored to the Church, and that they actually had been to his church.

A third factor was the violent rejection of the Pentecostal movement by almost the entire Protestant church, except some of the later Holiness denominations that went Pentecostal. But thanks be to God, this original violent prejudice against the Pentecostal experience and doctrine has greatly decreased. Today, 80 percent of all Christians in the Southern Hemisphere have had a Pentecostal experience with the Holy Spirit and His gifts.

A fourth factor was that Bible colleges and seminaries discriminated against Pentecostals and charismatics, not allowing them to attend if they spoke in tongues. But once again, things have been changing. Many schools that once would have refused Pentecostals or charismatics now allow them to enroll, and some have even hired professors who are charismatic or Pentecostal.

A fifth factor was that Protestant mission boards were firing missionaries who spoke in tongues or taught that the healing gifts were currently available for ministry. The Southern Baptist Mission Board officially adopted this position in 2007. (I will conclude this chapter shortly with an example of how this factor affected one missionary couple.)

A sixth factor was that denominations began disfellowshiping individual churches that began to have charismatic experiences such as speaking in tongues, falling under the power, having prophecies come forth or operating in healing ministries. Some of the largest churches in Asia and Brazil today were once Baptist, but were disfellowshiped when they began to have these experiences. One such church in

Manouse, Brazil, in which I have ministered multiple times, has 60,000 members in one congregation today. Another in Abidjan, Ivory Coast, has over 120,000 members. These are just two examples out of many similar stories.

A seventh factor, similar to one of the Catholic Church's factors, was that some Protestant denominations accommodated their charismatic pastors and people by allowing small groups and fellowships to form in the local churches, but they did not allow the worship services or liturgies to become charismatic in expression. This at least allowed charismatic people to remain in their local churches without being kicked out, and they could then develop a place where they could pray for each other, move in the gifts and worship with more abandon. But at the same time, these practices were isolated from the congregation at large.

This quarantine measure kept the charismata (gifts) out of congregational meetings while keeping charismatic members in the congregation. This compromising solution did not allow the Holy Spirit to have control in congregational worship services. There was no place for prophecies outside those quarantined charismatic groups. Neither was there a place for words of knowledge or gifts of healing, except in the condoned charismatic closets. In effect, the working of God through these gifts was relegated to places outside the experience of most members of a church. Though not quite a "don't ask—don't tell" policy, this served to keep charismatics in the closet.

I spoke to an official denomination's "charismatic fellowship" for a whole diocese a few years ago. Sadly, the movement of the Spirit—once so powerful and strong—had not been allowed to penetrate most of that body. As a result, almost everyone in attendance was gray headed. In the succeeding 25 years after the Spirit's outpouring, the ones who were initially touched still met to worship and pray for healings. But their institutional church life had not been impacted nearly as much as it could have been if the gifts of the Spirit had been more welcomed in the congregational services of the local churches.

An eighth and final factor was the moral failure of high-visibility leaders in Protestant healing ministries. Many people stopped believing in the message of healing these men brought because they stopped believing in the messengers when they fell into sin. We must remember, however, that it is not the *messenger* but the *message* itself that the Holy Spirit backs up and confirms. I believe those who fell were true men of God who, for different reasons, became self-deceived. Then they fell into self-deceptive thinking and next into self-destructive, sinful behavior that destroyed their ministries. At the end of these men's ministries, people were healed and saved even while the ministers themselves were in self-destruct mode.

## A Personal Example

Let me conclude this chapter with a story in which one of these factors greatly affected a couple's ability to minister effectively. The fifth Protestant church factor I mentioned was that Protestant mission boards began firing their missionaries who departed from the cessationist position. A few years ago, I met one such missionary couple personally while I was ministering in Imperatriz, Brazil, and they told me their story.

We had a substantial team with us numbering about eighty on the trip. I desperately needed more good translators to help us in our preaching and teaching, as well as helping when we prayed for the sick. An American family present was with a missionary sending agency that specialized in reaching unreached people groups. This family had pioneered a work among an indigenous people group. The father had started the work forty years ago and was now retired and in his eighties. His son and daughter-in-law and their teenage children were continuing his work. When I first met them, they were all cessationist, trained in this viewpoint. Yet we needed translators and they volunteered to help. They did not know what we believed when they agreed to come translate.

To this family's surprise, they found themselves translating our Gospel of the Kingdom messages that put forth the continued ministry of the Holy Spirit to bear witness to the Gospel through signs and wonders, healings and miracles. They also translated for us as we prayed for the sick and cast out demons. The father and mother, Dave and Diana, and the teenagers were all experiencing the reality of the Kingdom of God as they witnessed people being healed and set free day and night.

This created a theological crisis for Dave. He had taught that the gifts of healings and working of miracles no longer existed, but now he was seeing them happen right in front of his eyes. He began to seek God and study the Bible to see if these things were so. He came to believe his cessationist viewpoint was wrong. It was obvious that his doctrine and personal experience no longer quite lined up, and as he sought the Scriptures, he had a change of mind and heart.

At the conclusion of our trip, he asked if I would come to the hotel where he and his family were staying while they translated for us. I agreed, and when I arrived he told me that the whole family wanted me to lay hands on them and pray that there would be a transference from my life to theirs of the gifts of the Spirit. They also wanted the baptism with the Spirit. God answered my prayers by coming powerfully upon all of them. Rejoicing, we then went in different directions.

When our team returned to Imperatriz a year later, I heard the rest of their story. Dave and Diana had signed an agreement letter that if they ever left the mission agency for any reason, they would also leave the tribe and area they had been working with. Believing that exercising the gifts of the Spirit and speaking in tongues were tantamount to "leaving" the agency, they had to resign. So after we had left Brazil the first time, Dave duly wrote a letter of resignation and sent it to the leaders of his missions agency. This was extremely difficult for him because he and his family had all been born in Brazil and his father had pioneered their work among the indigenous people.

The day he sent the letter off, a genuine revival of classic character began. The Holy Spirit fell upon his church. Prior to this outpouring, the members had not been very excited about their faith. All ten of them would come late to the church—which met under a mango tree. They lacked passion in their worship, and around Dave and his family, they would often refer to God as "your God" rather than "our God."

This changed when the Holy Spirit fell. The church members became passionate for God. He was *their* God now. They wept under the conviction of the Holy Spirit due to the overwhelming presence of God's love. They would go door-to-door asking people they had wronged to forgive them. The tribe had built homes in a circular configuration, and the church members were going around the circle to make things right with other members of the tribe. Many whom they were visiting were not Christians, but were amazed by the changes in these Christians. Many therefore accepted Jesus.

Often, even before the Christians could get to all the homes, other tribal members were converted due to the powerful witness of the new converts. When the Christians heard someone was sick, they went and prayed for the person until he or she was healed. They also gave money toward going to other tribes with their message of revival. Other tribes soon heard about what was happening and came to see and experience it for themselves.

About this time, Dave's missions agency had just completed the New Testament in the language of the tribal people. This had taken almost forty years. When agency representatives arrived at Dave's church with the translations, they did not see the usual ten to fifteen Christians, but a crowd of over 200. They asked what all these people were doing at the church meeting. When Dave told them this was now the church, the missions agency representatives could scarcely believe it.

This story has a happy ending. When the agency leaders came to meet with Dave and Diana again to accept their resignation, about a year after they had sent the resignation letter, the representatives also met with the leaders of the tribe. The leaders told them that if they made Dave and Diana leave, the tribe did not want anyone else from the missions agency to come. Many did not want to return to the old religion—they wanted what was happening since the revival. In addition, the older chiefs of the village, who made the final decisions, were unwilling for the tribe to sever the strong ties of friendship with Dave and Diana. The missions agency therefore pulled out, deciding that if Dave and Diana stayed on as the pastors of the church, they no longer wished to be related to the church. The agency simply did not believe in modern-day healings or the other so-called sign gifts. Dave and his family, along with the tribal church his father had founded, parted ways amicably with the missions agency, preferring instead to continue growing in their newfound relationship with the Holy Spirit.

# 5

# HEALING AND THE KINGDOM

## *Bill*

God meant it when He said that He made the heavens for Himself, but the earth He made for man (see Psalm 115:16). God is still ruler over all things, but He delights in delegating responsibility to His creation. In doing so, He releases identity and purpose to all whom He created by giving them meaningful responsibilities. Placing Adam and Eve as His delegated authority over the planet was just such a move. God's intention was to rule over the earth in partnership with those He made in His image. Their assignment was simple: Live a productive life, have children who have children who have children, and subdue the earth from destructive and chaotic powers that run rampant outside the Garden (see Genesis 1:28). It was not that God would not rule here. In His sovereign plan, things just were not complete without people taking their place authoritatively through relationship with Him.

The Garden of Eden was a perfect place of divine order, but it was all Adam and Eve could manage with their population of two. As they increased in number and learned to manage what they were in charge of, they could extend the boundaries of the Garden until the entire planet was governed by God through His delegated ones—humankind.

Before the Garden and man were created, there were three archangels: Michael, Gabriel and Lucifer. Each of these created beings had responsibilities. Lucifer, now called the devil, was kicked out of heaven because of his rebellion. The Scriptures tell us that one third of the angels fell with him. It stands to reason that those who were under Lucifer's charge were the ones who left at the same time. The book of Revelation gives us an interesting insight into this event: "And his tail swept away a third of the stars of heaven and threw them to the earth" (Revelation 12:4). *Stars* may refer to the angelic realm who fell into rebellion, but the verse might also be saying that this event affected creation in that *stars* also were swept into their influence. Regardless, it is clear that the devil landed on earth. It also implies that the reason God chose earth from which to create man was to position him to take back the planet, the one place that was out of order in God's creation.

Since Satan wanted to be worshiped like God, God chose to overthrow Satan's dark kingdom through those He made in His image, who worshiped God by choice. God chose to defeat the devil and his cohorts through worshipers. Worship is the primary call of mankind. It is not an egotistical choice on God's part to give us that place in life. Love chooses the best. And considering that we always become like the One we worship, there is nothing better that God could desire for us.

I need to make one thing clear—at no time has the devil been a threat to God or the power of righteousness or His sovereign rule over all that is. God could easily destroy the devil with a breath. But as God, He chose to defeat him through humanity. A stunning plan, for sure.

God's plan did not fail. Adam and Eve did. They listened to the serpent's reasoning and became his possession (see Romans 6:16). Their place of dominion over creation, along with the keys of authority, also became his possession. That is why Satan could offer the realms of earthly authority to Jesus in the wilderness following His forty-day fast. The devil wanted to trade earthly dominion for what he had always wanted—worship (see Luke 4:6–7).

However, Jesus turned down all shortcuts to victory and God's redemptive plan kicked into gear. Jesus, God's only Son, became a man. As such, He would buy back humanity from its slave owner, the devil, while at the same time defeating that slave owner *as a man*! This fulfilled God's plan from the beginning. Everything we now do as believers is intended to reinforce and manifest the redemptive work and triumph over the powers of darkness that took place at Calvary. Jesus accomplished it all then and there.

The sacrificial death of Christ followed His perfectly lived life. It was essential that He face the same issues we do, but face them without sin—which He did. And He became the spotless Lamb, a sinless sacrifice removing the curse from man. When Jesus rose from the dead, He rose to rule. He declared, "All authority has been given to me!" (Matthew 28:18). If He has *all* authority, then the devil has *none*.

Jesus then gave His authority to those who would follow Him. He basically announced that we were back to *Plan A*: taking back the dominion of a planet, now as redeemed humankind.

### *Plan A* Made Simple

The first time the charge to govern the planet was given, Adam and Eve sinned by acting independently of God. Jesus came and modeled how carrying out this assignment is possible by following His lead and becoming the servant of all. We die to live, give to obtain, humble ourselves to be exalted . . . These are the attitudes and mindsets of another world, the world that is to have influence over this one. And to have true dominion over this world, our thought life must be conformed to that other world we represent.

Ours is a *relational* assignment. In other words, everything we are commanded to do is based on a present-tense relationship with God. The partnership is to demonstrate relationship. This is so very valuable to Him. To say that God needs us would be incorrect, of course. He is self-contained. He needs nothing. But He passionately desires to share His rule with those He made in His image, who worship Him by choice. Our assignment is simple: to follow our Master's lead and "destroy the works of the devil" (1 John 3:8).

This army of humankind meant to destroy the devil's works already fell once, in Adam. Independence from God was at the root of Adam's sin. He fell for the opportunity to "be like God." The strange part of the story is that he already was. Adam and Eve tried to get, through their own efforts of eating forbidden fruit, what they already had as a gift of God's grace. That was the painful Fall of man.

In Christ, our partnership to rule was restored. And just as importantly, He provided us with a model that illustrated how our assignment can be successfully carried out by being like Him. Christlikeness is our true goal as believers who are carrying out our job to preach and display the Gospel for what it is: Good News.

The commission to "take back the planet" starts with prayer. I do not mean a token prayer that we are sometimes guilty of, such as the prayer before a meal. I mean actual prayer that illustrates partnership. If my prayer does not move me, it will not move God. He shows us His will and then commands us to come into fellowship with Him and ask for the specifics of that will. Many people like to discuss the intricacies of prayer and often get distracted from the assignment to *pray*. It is His will for us to pray His will. Period.

It is foolish to assume that if something is God's will, it will automatically be done. That misconception is at the heart of powerless praying. Then prayer becomes a Christian activity that serves no real purpose other than to keep us occupied. Thinking God's will happens automatically is also a misconception about God's sovereignty. He *can* force His will easily. He has chosen not to. Partnership—co-laboring with us—is at the heart of His plan. And prayer is the initial part of our assignment.

Again, is His will always done? *No!* Consider 2 Peter 3:9, "The Lord is not slow about His promise, as some count slowness, but is patient toward you, not wishing for any to perish but for all to come to repentance." It is His will that none perish—yet people perish daily. We have a role to fulfill in carrying out His will. And the measure of His will that actually gets carried out is in some measure attached to how well we represent His purposes on the earth. We have a role, an influence, a part in the overall plan. We are partners with the divine.

When God tells us to pray in a particular way, it is not just to involve us in random Christian activity to make us feel useful. He is engaging us in the aforementioned partnership, where things get done properly and His will is released on the earth. Prayer is probably the most underrated of all Christian activities for that reason. It is the essential part that connects His heart with the actual circumstances of humanity. It is in that place of "agreement" where the heart of God is with the heart of man. That is what releases the purposes of God into the earth.

## The *Great* Prayer

Anointed prayers reveal the heart of God in powerful and unique ways. Scripture contains many such prayers, but none so revealing as what is commonly referred to as the Lord's Prayer. It contains the ultimate revelation of the will of God for our lives on this planet.

> Our Father who is in heaven,
> Hallowed be Your name.
> Your kingdom come.
> Your will be done,
> On earth as it is in heaven.
> Give us this day our daily bread.
> And forgive us our debts, as we also have forgiven our debtors.
> And do not lead us into temptation, but deliver us from evil.
> [For Yours is the kingdom and the power and the glory forever. Amen.]
>
> Matthew 6:9–13

This magnificent prayer has two basic parts: worship and petition. The petition has only one focus: the will of God. It deals with our need of provision, our relationships with God and others, and the issue of temptation. The language used here is critical in giving us a clear understanding of our assignment. "On earth as it is in heaven" is the key part of this prayer. It covers every realm of God's will for our lifetime.

Let's talk about the term *apostle* in relation to this prayer, a term that has almost been deified in recent years. It has become so elevated that the office has become untouchable—no one could ever qualify. While it is not my intention to deal with church government or the five-fold ministry in this book, it is important to use the term to help us understand the fuller meaning of the Lord's Prayer, the most famous prayer of all time.

The word *apostle* in the New Testament means "sent one." *Apostle* was originally a secular term used by both the Greeks and the Romans to refer to the leader of a special envoy. That leader had the job of establishing the culture of the empire he represented into the daily lives of the citizens the empire conquered. Leaders had discovered that the citizens of conquered lands went back to their previous way of life rather quickly without a transforming influence. It was extremely frustrating to see no change result in a conquered nation, which nullified the purpose of the conquest. For this reason, they came up with a strategy to transform the culture of a conquered city so that when the empire's leaders visited, it would feel the same as home. John Eckhardt's book, *Apostolic Ministry: A 50 Lesson Bible Course* (Crusaders Ministries, 2005) is a great reference for this subject. The position of apostle was created in response to this need. Jesus adopted the term to reveal His intentions. His apostles lead a special envoy of people who have the job of establishing the culture of the empire of heaven into the daily lives of the citizens they serve.

The Lord's Prayer is an apostolic prayer. *On earth as it is in heaven.* Make this world like that one. That does not mean you have to be an apostle to pray it. It means that the purpose of the prayer is a clear expression of the apostolic mandate to transform the thinking and lifestyles of the nation so that they are the same as the governing nation—in this case, heaven. This becomes the mandate of the Church when it has a full expression of healthy leadership. It astonishes me that we can spend so much of our Christian life doing everything but working to transform society. The hunger for heaven must stop making us irresponsible with this moment God has given us in history. The more the Church realizes who she is, the less she wants to be rescued. The Lord's return is beautiful and will be the ultimate culmination of events, but our assignment is not to go to heaven. It is to bring heaven to earth through prayer and obedience, by embracing the ministry of Jesus.

Healing was a major part of Jesus' ministry. There is no cancer in heaven. Neither is there any blindness or deafness or any other malady in that realm. Freedom from disease is God's will on earth. Period. God has not commanded us to pray for healing in order to frustrate us. Neither is prayer a spiritual exercise created to make us hungry for eternity. We are not to believe, *Physical health will never happen here; this can only happen in heaven. It is reserved as our eternal reward*. Heaven is meant to invade earth in this area.

Heaven invading earth is both simple and complex. It is simple in that every time someone is healed, converted or delivered, a piece of heaven has come upon them, destroying the devil's work. It is complex in the sense that the total ruling of heaven on earth is not accomplished through a moment of sincere petition. The diligent, relentless, focused prayer of a surrendered generation is what will accomplish this assignment.

## An Incomplete Message

For as long as I can remember, the message of the Church has been the salvation of souls. Wonderful evangelistic crusades are organized to bring the multitudes to Jesus. Evangelism is also taken to the streets, as normal people invade our cities and learn to share the good news of God's forgiveness for everyone. Perhaps it is the beauty of that message that has lulled us to sleep concerning the rest of our assignment. It is bigger than that. Jesus clearly taught us that we were to preach the message of the Kingdom to every nation before the end would come (see Matthew 24:14). That message releases the Kingdom through miracles.

The message of salvation is contained in the Gospel of the Kingdom. The good news of the Kingdom is the proclamation that God's dominion is in effect *now*. King-dom. That is, *King's domain*. The message of the Kingdom is the message of the King's domain that is in effect here and now. And whenever Jesus proclaimed this message, miracles followed. Miracles were the natural result of His dominion being realized. "Jesus was going through all the cities and villages, teaching in their synagogues and proclaiming the gospel of the kingdom, and healing every kind of disease and every kind of sickness" (Matthew 9:35). The right message attracts God's power since He loves to confirm His Word.

The message of salvation would not be so incomplete if it were preached as God intended. Today *salvation* means we can be "forgiven of sin." If there were nothing more than this, it would be worth it all. Forgiveness is still the ultimate miracle. But to assert that there is more to the message does not diminish the importance of forgiveness. It is just that God intended more. Jesus said, "For the Son of Man did not come to destroy men's lives, but to save them" (Luke 9:56). The word *save* in the original Greek language is the word *sozo*. It refers specifically to the *forgiveness* of sin, the *healing* of disease and the *deliverance* from torment. That is salvation. Jesus made the provision needed to save the whole person— spirit, soul and body:

- Spirit—forgiveness
- Soul—deliverance
- Body—healing

The Gospel of salvation is meant to touch the whole person. Another look at this truth comes from a study of the word *evil* as found in Matthew 6:13 (KJV), "Deliver us from evil." The word *evil* represents the entire curse of sin upon man. *Poneros* is the Greek word for evil. It came from the word *ponos*, which means "pain." And that word came from the root word *penes*, which means "poor." This is what Jesus came to destroy: evil-sin, pain-sickness and poor-poverty. Jesus destroyed the power of sin, sickness and poverty through His work at Calvary. Adam and Eve lived without sin, sickness and poverty in the Garden. Now that we are redeemed and restored to God's original purpose, should we expect anything less? Especially when what Jesus accomplished is called the better covenant?

Jesus our Savior came with dominion in mind. This was made clear: "For this purpose the Son of God was manifested, that He might destroy the works of the devil" (1 John 3:8, KJV). Since the works of the devil are often seen in the destruction evident in people's lives, it stands to reason that Jesus came to dethrone the enemy from his place of control and influence.

Today people usually get saved by repeating a prayer, but little else happens to them to establish them in a relationship with the One who truly set them free and made them new creations. These converts often live with torment and affliction, some for years, and some even for a lifetime. A fuller salvation at the beginning gives a person greater momentum into the relationship that God intended. Remember the man who was healed at the Gate Beautiful? Scripture tells us he walked, leaped and praised God. He was touched in every area. He was physically healed—he *walked*. He was emotionally healed—he *leaped*. He was also spiritually healed—he *praised* God. (See Acts 3:1–10.)

I remember some years ago giving an altar call one Sunday morning. Quite a few people came forward that day. One guy stood out. He was in great pain and had walked into the service with a cane. Disease had robbed him of the ability to walk without assistance. He was so moved with conviction to surrender to Christ that he responded quickly to go to the altar to pray with our prayer servants (which is what we call our altar workers). Only after he received Christ did he realize that he had left his cane back at his seat. He was actually healed as he came forward to receive the love of God in forgiveness. The salvation that wiped out the power of sin also destroyed the affliction in his body. He was saved, and there was nothing incomplete about it!

## Faith for Partial Salvation

Why do we have more faith for someone's conversion than we do for his or her healing? It is not biblical, but it is our experience. All of us tend to interpret the Scriptures according to our experience instead of pressing into the experience the Bible teaches about.

For centuries the Church has believed for people's conversions, and rightly so. That was brought to the front burner again in Martin Luther's day. But what would have happened if healing and deliverance had been included in the Church's definition of salvation, as it is in Scripture? I believe our faith for both realms would be similar. We are living in the momentum of accumulated faith for salvation—as it pertains solely to the forgiveness of sin. We have seen the verifiable results for generations. But when it has come to healing, one generation will pursue it while the next seems to drop the ball. No momentum is gained when each generation that pursues this part of the Gospel has to reinvent the wheel, so to speak. Healing brings conflict and much criticism. For that reason, this great subject gets abandoned as a pursuit, even though Paul states plainly to "desire earnestly spiritual gifts" (1 Corinthians 14:1). *Desire earnestly* actually means "to be jealous." This commandment is telling us that we are to *burn with zeal* in our pursuit of the "gifts of the Spirit." And healing is listed as one of those gifts.

Believing that healing is either not for today, or that it is not a part of our salvation, is a flat-out lie. Believing a lie empowers the liar. Coming into agreement with the devil by believing a lie enables him to steal from us that much more easily. When we ignore or deny what God has provided, we lose the ability to discern the realms of the Holy Spirit and often wind up attributing the devil's work to God.

The cost of tolerating lies is enormous. But spiritual false-hoods do not end with the lack of healing. Lies rob the heart of our natural ability to dream for more in our relationship with God. It makes fear king, while forcing us to live within the boundaries set by unbelief. While the quest for more of the miraculous makes many nervous, it is actually a sign of life. I refuse to listen to the warnings of possible excess from those satisfied with lack. The standard for the Christian life should not be set by those who have lost their ability to dream for the impossible. Pursuing the impossible is our nature in Christ.

## Now and Not Yet

*The Kingdom of God is both now and not yet.* That description was refreshing the first time I heard it. It seemed to give permission to pursue what God has made available, all the while reminding us that only heaven will give us access to everything. But of late the phrase has taken on a new meaning. It seems to be mentioned mostly by those who are afraid to pursue more, who need to feel comfortable with their lack of risk and are hoping that those around them will mirror the same apathy for the miraculous that they have. For them, it explains why some things we pray for do not happen. When the disciples did not get a supernatural breakthrough as they were accustomed to, they asked Jesus why (see Mark 9:28). He explained that sometimes we need to add fasting and prayer to our pursuit. In other words, some realms in God will not be brought to us—they must be pursued.

Whenever we create a theology around what *did not* happen, we always fall short of God's plan. His intentions are beyond the reach of both our prayer life and our imagination (see Ephesians 3:20). So the question remains, how much of the Kingdom can we have in this lifetime? No one knows for sure. Our physical bodies could not stand a full manifestation of His glory; we would disintegrate. But history tells us that previous generations have lived with measures of breakthrough beyond what we presently see. And considering that God wants to take us beyond His own measure of breakthrough, we fall short of John 14:12, "Truly, truly, I say to you, he who believes in Me, the works that I do, he will do also; and greater works than these he will do; because I go to the Father." We must not settle for any level we are comfortable with. That is a sure sign of spiritual anemia. Discomfort makes room for the Comforter. I tend to think He will let us have as much as our bodies can handle.

The apostle Paul was devoted to preaching the Gospel of the Kingdom (see Acts 28:31). But he made it clear that it involved more than words. The Kingdom was then and is now made manifest in power. The good news of God's world invading this one must be preached with power in order to deal with the infirmities of man. The Gospel was never intended to be a message solely about what we will have access to after we die. It is a *right now* message.

Look at Romans 15:18–19: "For I will not presume to speak of anything except what Christ has accomplished through me . . . in the power of signs and wonders, in the power of the Spirit . . . I have fully preached the gospel of Christ." To fully preach this good news of the Gospel requires power, for without power it is no longer good news. The Gospel must include miracles to be fully expressed. Miracles are not optional.

When the church in Rome was placing undue value on the natural realm, Paul corrected their perspective with the following statement: "For the kingdom of God is not eating and drinking, but righteousness and peace and joy in the Holy Spirit" (Romans 14:17). Righteousness, peace and joy are clear manifestations of the Kingdom of God. And in a very real sense, they reveal the intended reach or purpose of salvation:

- Righteousness—answers the sin issue (spirit)
- Peace—answers the torment issue (soul)
- Joy—answers the affliction issue (body)

Joy is a Kingdom expression. Fullness of joy exists in God's presence (see Psalm 16:11). And although joy has value in theory, it is often offensive in practice since joy sometimes manifests in laughter. Weeping in a service is not only acceptable to many; it is accepted as evidence that God is working powerfully. Laughter is not necessarily seen in the same light. Weeping is often an expression of repentance, but laughter is an expression of joy. And what weeping is to repentance, laughter is to salvation. Solomon explains the physical body's response to joy when he states, "A joyful heart is good medicine" (Proverbs 17:22). Joy has a healing effect on the body and mind. And as a Kingdom manifestation, it is priceless.

## Jesus Reflected Perfect Theology

Jesus came to an orphaned planet to reveal the Father. That was something that neither the Law nor the Prophets could do. Everything changed in that one revelation of Jesus—Jesus revealed the Father. For the first time, people were able to see both an accurate and a complete picture of God's heart toward them. What was seen in type and shadow under the Old Covenant is now seen clearly through Jesus Christ.

Jesus reflected perfect theology both in what He showed us of the Father and what He showed us about carrying out the Father's will. Jesus emptied Himself of divinity and became man (see Philippians 2:7). While He is eternally God, He chose to live within the restrictions of a man who had no sin and was empowered by the Holy Spirit. In doing this, He provided a compelling model for us to follow.

While it can truthfully be said that Jesus did not heal everyone alive in His day, it must also be noted that He healed everyone who came to Him. No exceptions. The measures of faith people expressed varied, from *if you are able*, to *if you are willing*, to *just touch us*, to *let me touch you* to finally *just say the word* (see Mark 9:22; Mark 1:40; Matthew 9:29; Mark 6:56; Matthew 8:8). Jesus responded to great faith and little faith. The father who said *if you are able* hardly registers

125

on faith's Richter scale, yet his faith was enough to bring Jesus the Healer to the forefront once again. He healed that father's child.

A major change in theology has taken place over the past two thousand years. When Jesus walked the earth, all sickness was from the devil. Today a large part of the Body of Christ believes God either sends sickness or allows it to make us better people by building character and teaching us the value of suffering. If God allows sickness, can we still call the devil a thief? After all, if the thief has permission to steal, it is no longer called stealing. Yet Acts 10:38 tells us "God anointed Jesus of Nazareth with the Holy Spirit and with power, who went about doing good and healing all who were oppressed by the devil, for God was with Him" (NKJV).

This same group who believes God sends sickness also considers those who pray for the sick to be deceived by the devil, or at least be "out of balance." Somewhere in today's theology, God took over the devil's job! The early Church knew that the devil came to steal, kill and destroy, but now the Church gives God the blame. If God truly sent sickness, we would interfere with His great plan by going to a doctor. Of course, this is nonsense. But this change in theology has had its influence in much of the Church. And as we do with any other sin, we need to confess and repent of it. Repentance means to change the way we think. Sorrow over such a sin of misrepresenting God to others must bring about a change in how we view reality. Renewing our minds through repentance will go a long way in getting out of this hole of unbelief and deception. Remember, healing is not just something God does. It is who He is. His name is Jehovah Rapha, *the God who heals* (see Exodus 15:26). To deny this is to deny the nature of God, who never changes.

Jesus healed all disease. He accurately and properly represented the Father by demonstrating His love through power.

126

If we have money but turn our backs on the cry of the poor, people have reason to question our walk with God. But if we have the Spirit of the resurrected Christ living in us and turn our backs on the cry of the sick, are we any less guilty? I think not.

Jesus started His ministry with a statement that would completely define our lives: "Repent, for the kingdom of heaven is at hand" (Matthew 4:17). In other words, *change the way you think, for I brought My world with Me. And unless you change your perspective on life, you can live within reach of all that you long for, but never taste of its reality.*

# 6

# HEALING AND THE AUTHORITY
# OF THE BELIEVER

*Bill*

Jesus said, "My food is to do the will of Him who sent me" (John 4:34). The will of God nourished and strengthened Jesus. It should be no different for us. Any time we emphasize the difficulty of obeying God's will above the rewards and fruits of carrying it out, we take a victim's approach to obedience. God's will is glorious. Jesus experienced great joy because of His love for all that was right. Speaking of Jesus, the Bible said, "You have loved righteousness and hated lawlessness; therefore God, Your God, has anointed You with the oil of gladness more than Your companions" (Hebrews 1:9, NKJV). Jesus illustrated the pleasure and benefit of doing the Father's will.

Jesus' love of righteousness was matched by His hatred of lawlessness. Even though it cost Him His life, God's only Son did the will of the Father and sacrificed Himself to destroy the powers of darkness over all of mankind. Sometimes what we love is measured by what we hate. In hating what God hates and loving what God loves, we are positioned to discover the pleasure of His will, for God only hates whatever interferes with love.

We were born into a spiritual war against the powers of darkness Jesus gave His life to conquer. The war is not against our doctrines or our Christian organizations, as much as it is against our ability to demonstrate the reality of the resurrection through miracles, signs and wonders. There is no question that anyone who ministers in the anointing will face opposition and conflict. The antichrist spirit is at work in the world. Christ means *anointed one*. That antichrist spirit always works against the anointing. That is the target: the anointing that enables every believer to demonstrate the works of Jesus in our day. The conflict we all face should not be a surprise. But to emphasize the price we pay above the rewards is to bring attention to ourselves more than to the One who gives us the grace to pay the price—who also rewards those who seek Him. "And without faith it is impossible to please Him, for he who comes to God must believe that He is and that He is a rewarder of those who seek Him" (Hebrews 11:6). Believing in God's nature as a rewarder is a mandated expression of our faith. To revel in the pain of obedience instead of its reward is a perversion.

## Watching God Work

Learning to hear God's voice and follow His lead is joyful and exciting, yet I must admit it also keeps me on edge. I was at Grace Center, a great church outside Nashville, when a woman came to me for prayer. She was afflicted with rheumatoid arthritis head to toe. As I moved to pray for her, I felt a check in my heart that I was not to pray. Yet I could also tell Jesus was going to heal her. Just as our computers have "default" settings with preselected fonts and the like, so I have a default approach to praying for the sick. I find out what is wrong, lay my hands on the person and invite the Holy Spirit to come with power and glorify the name of Jesus through His healing touch. I do that when I do not sense another direction. But in this case, something was different. It felt as though I would interfere with the work of God if I prayed or laid hands on her. I was not even allowed to make decrees of healing over her or pronounce her well, as Jesus did with, "Go your way; the demon has gone out of your daughter" (Mark 7:29, NKJV).

This woman's healing was to be a school of the Spirit for me, and I assume for her as well. I asked her to close her eyes so that the other ministry going on around the room would not distract her. She did as I requested. Then I sensed a heat on the back of my neck, obvious but subtle. It felt like hot oil slowly flowing downward, so I told her the anointing was flowing down her neck. She said she felt it. When it reached the base, I told her the neck should be healed by now. She moved it about in ways that would have caused pain before, only to find that it was, in fact, healed.

In that moment I realized what God was doing. I was a play-by-play announcer, like at a sporting event. It was my privilege to describe what God was doing in her as He showed me on my own body. He wanted to heal her without it flowing through me either through prayer, decree or the laying on of hands. It is important for us to understand that it is always God who heals. Sometimes we get to deliver the package (gift). Sometimes we watch Him deliver the package Himself.

For me, that kind of healing is one of the most special moments in healing ministry. The hot oil continued to flow down her shoulders with the same outcome. From there it moved down the spine to the tailbone. Each time, I would describe what God was touching. And each time, she acknowledged that she felt the same thing. She would move about, testing the area that God had been touching, each time finding that God had completely healed that area. We followed this pattern until the healing reached her toes, where we were able to give thanks for a complete and total healing. This happened without anyone even praying for her. I love being used by God to give a word of knowledge describing what He is healing or to lay hands on someone for a miracle. But my favorite thing is to watch God at work without my doing anything but observing and rejoicing.

So much is already within reach—*at hand*. We tend to want to pray for what we already possess and do something to bring it about. And all too often, we ask God to do what He has already decided to do. As Randy Clark says, "To beg God to heal is to assume you have more mercy than He does." God has already decided to heal people, and He demonstrated that choice by purchasing the miracle with the stripes on Jesus' body.

## Letting the Father Lead

Jesus only did what the Father was doing and only said what the Father was saying (see John 5:17–18; 8:26). This sets a pretty high standard for how to live. While Jesus is eternally God, He emptied Himself of His divinity and became a man (see Philippians 2:7). It is vital to note that He did all His miracles as a man, not as God. If He did them as God, I would still be impressed. But because He did them as a man

132

yielded to God, I am now unsatisfied with my life, being compelled to follow the example He has given us. Jesus is the only model for us to follow.

No two miracles of Jesus recorded in Scripture were done in exactly the same way. I cannot help but wonder if our tendency to get locked into patterns and principles, though they have value, might work against our need to stay connected to *what the Father is doing*. It is no longer a question of whether it is God's will to heal. Now it is only a question of *how*.

Developing an ear for His voice seems to be at the heart of this issue, for faith comes by hearing, not having heard (see Romans 10:17). Faith implies a present-tense relationship with God. What we know can keep us from what we need to know if we do not stay childlike in our approach to life and ministry. Past success is often what prevents us from greater success. Our first breakthrough came because we heard from God, but when we create a pattern out of what we last heard, we create a problem. The key for Jesus was not putting mud in a man's eye or telling him to wash in the pool of Siloam (see John 9:6–7). It was not the action done. It was hearing the voice of the Father and doing what He said that made that particular act powerful. As Luke 4:4 says, we live by every word that proceeds from God's mouth.

We can see how the Father directed Jesus to do certain things to bring a breakthrough. Whether it was the spit that Jesus put on the mute man's tongue or simply saying to the centurion, "Go; it shall be done for you as you have believed," Jesus acted from the Father's direction (see Mark 7:33; Matthew 8:13). But what about the woman who touched Jesus' clothing? Or what about the Syrophoenician woman who wanted her daughter healed, even though Jesus said the time was not right because He needed to minister to the Jew first? (See Matthew 9:21; Mark 7:24–30.) The Father did not direct

Jesus to either of them, yet in both cases Jesus recognized the Father's gift of faith functioning in them and brought the breakthrough they cried out for—one before the fact, the other after.

It greatly encourages and helps me to see through these examples that God's *will* is not always made known to us directly. Sometimes we must learn to recognize what He is doing by watching how people respond to the Holy Spirit. Knowledge of His will is always available for those who want to see it. It is a very important part of the "normal Christian life" of signs, wonders and miracles.

## Presence and the Power of Boldness

We can expect miracles when we face the impossible. He is with us for that purpose. We know that the Holy Spirit is our guide, comforter and teacher. But His presence is made manifest through the impossibilities of life bowing to the name of Jesus through our lips. To embrace anything less than this is to miss the purpose of God's promise, "I will be with you." His presence enables us to change the world around us.

Acts 10:38 says, "You know of Jesus of Nazareth, and how God anointed Him with the Holy Spirit and with power, and *how* He went about doing good and healing all who were oppressed by the devil, *for God was with Him*" (emphasis added). Jesus healed all who came to Him, for God was with Him. It was *cause and effect*: Healing was the expected result because God was with Him. It cannot get much simpler than that. When God's presence was revealed upon or with someone, it was expected that miracles would follow. In fact, whenever God said, "I will be with you," it was because He had just given an impossible assignment. The Great Commission is a perfect example. Jesus promised to be with these new believers whom He had just commissioned to do the impossible: disciple the nations (see Matthew 28:19–20). The promise is now passed on to us as those who have received the same assignment. His presence has purpose, an intended effect—His miracles are to transform the world around us!

The Holy Spirit in us is the same Holy Spirit who raised Jesus from the dead. He is *the* Spirit of the resurrected Christ. When He took up residence in us, all of heaven positioned itself to see what we would conquer in His name. This is the fruit of being a *believing* believer, not an unbelieving believer of the kind Randy talked about back in chapter 4. Transformation of the world around us is the expected result of carrying His presence.

As I said in the previous chapter, if as a wealthy man I turn my back on the cry of the poor, you have reason to question my relationship with God. If as a spiritually wealthy man (filled with the Holy Spirit) I turn my back on the cry of the sick, am I any less guilty? The Spirit *without measure* is in me. He has all the gifts needed to make me successful. Likewise, He makes all of us spiritually wealthy. It was the presence of the Holy Spirit upon Jesus that made it possible for Him to heal the sick and raise the dead. The anointing that qualified Him, qualifies me (see John 5:19; Exodus 40:15; Luke 4:18–19).

A bold confession of faith is what often attracts the miracle into a given situation. "And they went out and preached everywhere, while the Lord worked with them, and *confirmed the word* by the signs that followed" (Mark 16:20, emphasis added). God confirms His word through miracles, signs and wonders. As 1 Corinthians 4:20 says, "The Kingdom of God is not a matter of talk but of power" (NIV). The bold declaration of the Gospel of the Kingdom brings the God of miracles to the forefront: "Now, Lord, look on their threats, and grant to Your servants that *with all boldness they may speak Your word*, by stretching out Your hand to heal, and that signs and wonders may be done through the name of Your holy Servant Jesus" (Acts 4:29–30 NKJV, emphasis added).

One of the more encouraging things I have experienced as a pastor is seeing believers respond differently to crises than they used to. It is seldom now a reaction of fear or panic. Instead, many have learned to make a bold confession of God's nature, feed their heart on His promises and boast in His absolute goodness.

## Power and Authority

Jesus gave His disciples power and authority to minister as He did. "Then He called His twelve disciples together and gave them *power* and *authority* over all demons, and to cure diseases. He sent them to preach the kingdom of God and to heal the sick" (Luke 9:1–2, NKJV, emphasis added). According to *Biblesoft's New Exhaustive Strong's Numbers and Concordance with Expanded Greek-Hebrew Dictionary* (Biblesoft and International Bible Translators, 1994, 2003), the words *power* and *authority* in the original Greek are translated:

> *Power:* **dunamis** (doo'-nam-is); miraculous power (usually by implication, a miracle itself) [NT:1411]

> *Authority:* **exousia** (ex-oo-see'-ah); privilege, superhuman, token of control, delegated influence or authority, jurisdiction, liberty, power, right [NT:1849]

These two realms are heaven's influence for life and ministry. Both realms are necessary to enable us to be instant in season and out. They are, in fact, a two-edged sword that enables us to be much more effective, regardless of the circumstances.

I like to compare ministering in *power* to a surfer catching a wave. We position ourselves in ministry, look for what God is doing and paddle like crazy to catch the wave. It is a great privilege to experience those moments. In fact, it is a lifelong journey for me to learn to ride the manifestation of His power.

I remember one Sunday night I felt the *healing presence of Jesus* come into the room. I stopped in the middle of what I was saying and announced what I felt, pointing to the back part of the sanctuary, where He entered. (It is a bit awkward trying to describe something that *you know that you know that you know* when you cannot give the kind of language to it that would be the most benefit to others. I saw it, but not with my eyes.) When the words came out of my mouth, a man with prostate cancer was immediately healed. No one prayed over him. The pain just left. His doctor verified his healing that week. A woman with a breast tumor was healed, too. When her friend heard my decree, she reached her hand over and touched this lady's shoulder. The tumor disappeared. Many others were impacted by the presence to heal. (See Luke 5:17).

All I did was spot the wave, change the course of the meeting (paddle to catch it) and announce what I saw (catch the wave.) The result was obvious: Jesus confirmed His Word with power. I love this journey with Jesus through the Holy Spirit. It is one adventure after another—and always a learning process.

Authority is quite different than power. Power is explosive and environmental in the sense that it is the actual atmosphere of heaven that changes the atmosphere of earth. Authority is a position given by Jesus Himself. A policeman carries a gun (power), but he also carries a badge (authority). The badge does much more than the gun.

Power is the atmosphere of heaven. Ministering in power is like catching a wave. Authority is like starting a wave. Things start happening because of who God says we are and what our responsibilities are. Faith is what connects us to this realm of authority—we have to believe what He says about us and what He has commissioned us to do.

One of our young men, Brandon, went down to a local bar on his twenty-first birthday, but not to celebrate in the usual worldly way. He spotted other young men in the back and went over to start a conversation. As he began to talk with one of them, the Lord showed him something about the young man's life that He wanted to heal. The Spirit of God came upon the young man, who then called a friend over to their booth to experience the same thing. Brandon turned to the young man with a word of wisdom about how to handle certain things in his relationship with his father. This came through a word of knowledge. That young man began to weep. He then told Brandon, "I want to buy you a drink!" When he turned him down, saying he was not there to drink, the tearful young man asked him, "Then what are you here for?"

Brandon responded, "I'm here for you."

Now, recognize that there was no great worship team helping set the atmosphere of God's presence in the bar. Neither was there a stirring sermon to help people believe God for the impossible. There was not even the faith-charged atmosphere that happens when believers are gathered in agreement. There was just darkness invaded with light: a single light. But it was enough.

## The New Norm

It has become normal for us to see miracles in public places simply because of this thing called authority. In fact, many of the greatest miracles we have ever seen have come from this privileged position—the deaf hearing, a deaf-mute hearing and speaking, many empty wheelchairs, cancer leaving in the aisle of a store and many other amazing miracles, too many to list. Learning to act out of *who we are* to God is central to success in the realm of miracles. It is called *authority*.

This definition of ministering in authority is not a contradiction to ministering in power, which is best represented by the challenge to *do only what you see the Father do*. Sometimes the only way to find out what the Father is doing is to use your authority to get there. Some have been poisoned with a view of God's sovereignty that has robbed the Church of human responsibility and purpose. One of the great mistakes made in history was of a major church leader who refused any involvement in supporting missions to a godless nation. His position was, "If God wants those people saved, He doesn't need our help. He can save them without us." Technically that is true, in that God can do anything. But in this case, it is a violation of His revealed will and therefore works against the sovereignty it tries to protect. He has written our involvement, and even our desires, into His sovereign plan.

## What about Now?

Previous to the moment in Luke 9:1–2 when Jesus gave His disciples power and authority, they had been operating under the *umbrella* of His anointing and call. I experienced something similar to this, but on a much smaller scale, with our dear friend Dick Mills.

Dick has memorized over 7,700 promises of the Bible in various translations. He is known for profound prophetic ministry using Scriptures. It is an unusual and amazing gift that brings so much encouragement to people, even those who do not believe in the prophetic ministry for today. It is hard for people to reject Dick's ministry because he just uses Scripture.

My family and I went to spend a day with Dick and his wife, Betty. Since there was a meeting that night, we decided to stay and enjoy gleaning from his unusual gift. When Dick was finished with his message, he told the people that he was going to call individuals to the front and give them prophetic words from Scripture. He then told them he would hand the microphone to me and I would do the same thing. Dick had never discussed this with me! I was terrified inside, but I obeyed. It was amazing. I stepped into Dick's gift and functioned as he did under his anointing by honoring his gift and yielding to his direction. His gift increased my own capacity to minister.

In much the same way, the disciples functioned under Jesus' anointing, but not for an evening, as in my story, but for three and a half years. When Jesus died, things had to change for their benefit. Now they would need their own experience with God. Following the resurrection, the disciples received an upgraded assignment and authority from the resurrected One. This comes to us in two passages:

> And Jesus came up and spoke to them, saying, "All authority has been given to Me in heaven and on earth. Go therefore and make disciples of all the nations, baptizing them in the name of the Father and the Son and the Holy Spirit, teaching them to observe all that I commanded you; and lo, I am with you always, even to the end of the age."
>
> Matthew 28:18–20

> So Jesus said to them again, "Peace be with you; as the Father has sent Me, I also send you."
>
> John 20:21

The One with authority had now commissioned the remaining eleven disciples with His authority. Death, sin and the powers of darkness had been defeated. From that triumph, they were called to accelerate what they had already been doing for these few years. But now they were to do so by giving witness to the resurrection itself, announcing the forgiveness of sin that was available to all.

One thing remained undone. The disciples were given the *exousia* (authority), as we saw in Luke 9, but what about the *dunamis* (power)? The disciples were also given authority in the Great Commission, but Jesus now required that they not leave Jerusalem until they had received the *dunamis*—power from on high:

> And behold, I am sending forth the promise of My Father upon you; but you are to stay in the city until you are clothed with power from on high.
>
> Luke 24:49

> Gathering them together, He commanded them not to leave Jerusalem, but to wait for what the Father had promised.
>
> Acts 1:4

Jesus was clothed with the power of the Holy Spirit at His own water baptism, where as a man, He had His personal encounter with the Holy Spirit (see Luke 3:22; John 1:32). Now the disciples would need the same.

Today, everyone who receives Christ is given authority. "But as many as received Him, to them He gave the right to become children of God, even to those who believe in His name" (John 1:12). The word *right* in this verse is the word *exousia*, or *authority*—meant for us all. And today the command remains the same for us as for the disciples tarrying in Jerusalem: We ought not leave our ministry base until we are clothed with *dunamis*—power from on high.

# Part 3

# THE PRACTICE OF HEALING

We discuss how to walk out the ministry of healing in both the Church and in personal life. We look at cultivating a culture of faith, moving into health with a prosperous soul and the vital importance of keeping the testimony. We also talk about words of knowledge and how to receive them, and then present the Five-Step Prayer Model in detail, along with practical examples of how to apply the model at every step.

# 7

# CREATING A FAITH CULTURE

*Bill*

Several years ago, I was in an all-day prayer meeting that left an indelible mark on my life. While there, I met Mike Servello, a pastor from Utica, New York. We had corresponded through email but had never met in person.

While the worship team was playing, Mike leaned over to me and said, "God is looking for a city that would belong entirely to Him. And once He gets that one city, it will cause a domino effect across our nation."

I told him I believed my city, Redding, California, was that city. He said he believed Utica, New York, was. In print it may look like a competition. It was not. It was two pastors expressing their faith for the big picture.

A little while later, I was in a different part of the sanctuary. Standing next to me was a friend and prophetic lady named Jean Krisle. She turned to me and said, "God is looking for a city that would belong entirely to Him. And once He gets that one city, it will cause a domino effect across our nation."

I was stunned. It was word for word what Mike had declared maybe thirty minutes earlier. Before I could mention my convictions for my city, she said, "And I believe Redding is that city."

It is not about one city being better than another. It is about each of us fully utilizing the resources God has made available to us to complete our assignment well. We are not in a race against each other. We are in a race against time.

The best way to create an atmosphere of faith is to start with an overwhelming awareness of need and realize the impossibility of our assignment from God. Often we get caught up with what is possible through human effort. We build our buildings and pay for great programs. While those things are good, it is tragic when they become the high point of our celebration of Christian achievement. When that is the case, it makes us no different than one of the many good service clubs in our communities. We are responsible for more. We are responsible to live in such a way that the Gospel that Jesus lived, preached and demonstrated will once again take center stage in world affairs. The impossible invites the faith-*full* to come and conquer.

Our dear friend Heidi Baker, of Iris Ministries, is known for her passion to *stop for the one*, as she puts it. We must not get so focused on big numbers that we forget the individual. Yet we must also remember that ministry to the one sets us up for the transformation of cities and nations. Being overwhelmed with the task at hand should take us quickly to the end of our resources—which is the beginning of His resources. Faith is the primary tool used to access and release all that He has made available. This is no small matter. Jesus said the Father had given Him *everything* as an inheritance.

It is the Holy Spirit who transfers *everything* to our account through His declarations (see John 16:14–16). Every time He speaks, a deposit is made into our account that enables us to complete our commission.

Since God is not a God of waste, why would He give us *all things*? Because the size of our assignment is that big. We will need to learn how to utilize *all things* that God has given us to succeed at societal transformation. His gifts are not casual or unintentional.

## Our DNA

It is said that when a kernel of corn is planted, every kernel that grows on a resulting ear of corn has the exact same DNA as the original kernel in the ground. Jesus became the ultimate seed that was *planted* in death, and we were born again by the same Spirit that raised Him from the dead. Every born-again believer has the DNA of Christ. That is amazing!

This DNA of Christ in us is practical in that it enables the Godlike capacity to dream. Life is not focused on the significance of our gifts or calling, or even our human talents or our faith. It is about the significance of the investment Jesus made—He was planted to redeem people *unto* something. And that *unto* something involves accurately and fully representing who Jesus is on earth as in Heaven. We have His DNA and therefore manifest His face to the world. This is not a pipe dream. It is the most practical ambition possible: to accurately represent Him to the world. It is part of God's eternal purpose for humanity.

I wish we would realize how born again we actually are. One of the things that becomes evident in the life of a believer is his or her appetite for the impossible. It is normal for a believer to have faith, yet the subject has become so complicated that many do not even think it is practical for them to really live a life of faith. It is! It is as much a part of our DNA as it was for Jesus. In fact, the only way believers would *not* desire for the impossible to bow to Jesus' name through their lips is if they have had bad teaching. Such teaching can deaden their hearts to that desire. Or they may have experienced disappointment that stays unresolved at redemption. I believe such disappointment has had far more lasting effects on people than bad teaching, as destructive as that is. People with bad doctrine are always one experience away from a transformed view of life. But unless resolved, disappointment is a cancer that grows until it takes the life of its host. (Later in this chapter, we will talk about how to prevent this when I discuss the steps involved in healing disappointed hearts.)

Many great men and women of God have both received and given bad teaching on miracles and faith. Strangely, much of it comes from a passion for the Scriptures. But it exists without the tension of an equal passion for the Holy Spirit, who inspired the Scriptures.

Frequently people ask me, "What do we do if we pray for someone and they are not healed?" It is in my DNA now to want everyone healed, but quite honestly, not everyone I pray for gets healed. The thing to remember is that the lack is never on God's side of the equation. We have to make sure that we do not turn people who need a miracle into our projects. These people are not a notch to put on the back of our Bibles once they are healed. They are individuals who must know the love of God. That is our privilege—to make sure they know God's love, as shown by our compassion for them in their difficulty. This compassion must become practical as we learn how to pursue the manifestation of a miracle in their lives.

For compassion to be practical and biblical, it has to take us into boldness. If it does not, then what we are feeling is probably closer to sympathy—compassion's counterfeit. Sympathy acknowledges the existence of a problem, but cannot offer answers or solutions. With it we show people we care, but we become more inclined to help people with coping skills rather than bring deliverance. Jesus did not train Seeing Eye dogs for the blind or build crutches for the lame. Compassion led Him into a breakthrough—every single time He was moved with compassion, the end result was a miracle. Compassion has its focus and anchor in the nature of God and His purposes for humanity.

## The Culture of Faith

Faith *pursues*. The nature of faith is reflective of God's nature. Part of the definition of faith is believing that God is a *rewarder*: "And without faith it is impossible to please Him, for he who comes to God must believe that He is and that He is a rewarder of those who seek Him" (Hebrews 11:6). It is not good enough to believe that God exists or that He can even perform the miracle I need. The devil believes those things. Faith lives out of the revelation of God's nature as a rewarder!

The following is a list of things that I have done and still do to increase my personal experience in faith and the experience of the church I pastor. I have learned that much of what we need in life is brought to us, but most of what we want, we have to go get. That is the divine purpose of continuous pursuit.

**1. Cry Out to God**—Be specific and passionate in pursuing miracle breakthroughs. Paul said to pursue earnestly spiritual gifts. We are not to assume they will simply function in our lives without the element of passionate prayer.

I have learned to take note of the seasons when many people come to me with the same disease by learning to contend for a breakthrough with that affliction. I take the *coincidence* as a *summons* from the Lord to obtain a breakthrough anointing for that disease.

Prayers that do not move me will not move God. While He does not forget His promises, reminding Him brings us into line with His covenant revealed in His Word. I do not know any way to put it more simply than learning to cry out to God in the secret place and taking risks in the public place. When the miracle comes, we give thanks, giving God all the glory. When it does not, we return to the secret place and make our requests known to God. Prayer with fasting is an important part of this process, as it was the counsel of Jesus to His disciples when they did not see the miracle they were pursuing (see Mark 9:14–29).

The final part of this directive is to learn to pray in the Spirit continuously. It is the one main ingredient given in Scripture for building our faith (see Jude 20).

**2. Bible Study**—The Scriptures reveal how the Holy Spirit moves. We especially see how He moves through the life of Jesus. For that reason, I pore over the Gospels and Acts. Jesus' teaching on the Kingdom contains much insight for us in this regard. But it is hard to recognize an answer if I do not have the question. Hunger is necessary. It is the continuous pursuit that changes the pursuer. All true study is driven by hunger. If you do not have questions, you will not recognize the answers.

Look for models to follow from Scripture. Look especially at all references to the Kingdom, and ask God to open the mysteries of the Kingdom to you. The right to understand such things belongs to saints who are willing to obey. Another great place for study is to find all references to "reformation," those periods of transformation that Israel went through under different leaders (revivalists) in the Scriptures. Good places to begin are with David, Hezekiah, Ezra and Nehemiah. Their lives become prophetic messages for us.

**3. Research History**—Find books written by the generals of God's army—those who have lived or are living the supernatural lifestyle. A great storehouse of information awaits those willing to pursue. Do not forget the leaders of the great healing revival of the 1950s. The book series *God's Generals* by Roberts Liardon is a great place to start (Whitaker House, 2003, 2008, 2011).

We cannot be afraid of including the stories of people who did not end well. Many such leaders were powerfully used by God before their failures. If you are afraid to read about those who later fell into sin and deception, then you will have to stay away from the stories of Gideon and Samson, and not read Solomon's Proverbs or the Song of Solomon. God has never been embarrassed to tell the whole story. Sometimes the lesson we need most is in the life of one whose ending is an embarrassment. We must learn to eat the meat and throw out the bones.

**4. Impartation**—Pursue the men and women of God who live a miracle lifestyle and ask them to lay hands on you and pray. You can obtain a grace for miracles in this way. This is one of the things that the apostle Paul taught (see 1 Timothy 4:14). This is not the only way to receive an impartation, though. Sometimes we can receive it through the influence of their ministry and the heart of honor we cultivate for the Holy Spirit upon them and the gift they carry. And remember, gifts are free, but maturity is expensive.

**5. Associations**—The story of David and Goliath is one of the best-known Bible stories in the world. Yet few people realize that at least four other giants were killed in the Bible—all by men who were followers of David. If you want to kill giants, hang around a giant killer. It rubs off.

Grace is that which enables us to live a Kingdom lifestyle. In part, we receive it based on how we respond to the gifts of Christ: apostles, prophets, evangelists, pastors and teachers. We receive enablement *to function* by honoring these gifts. If you develop a relationship with an evangelist, you will think evangelistically. The same happens when you associate with those who regularly experience signs and wonders in their lives. It rubs off.

6. **Obedience**—We pray and obey, and we learn to make room for God. He is the extravagant one. We simply make room for Him to do what He does by nature: heal and restore. Radical obedience—a life of risk—is needed for continual breakthrough in miracles, signs and wonders. Because of my special hatred for cancer, I have determined to look for people with that affliction. I learned a long time ago that more people are healed when I pray for more people! Until we act on what we know, our knowledge is nothing more than a theory. Real learning comes through doing.

7. **Stewardship**—One of the primary principles of the Kingdom is that *increase comes through use.* Correctly stewarding what God gives us is the way we obtain more. Sometimes the Lord answers us in seed form, knowing that proper stewardship is what prepares us for the increase we have asked for.

## Obstacles to Getting Started

Christians who ignore Jesus' command to heal the sick often wake up to the need for it when a family member or close friend becomes ill. I am thankful that God can use such crises to bring us back to His will. But praying for family is the hardest place to start in learning this lifestyle of miracles, signs and wonders. If you find yourself in such a position, do not lose heart. Just realize the challenge involved in praying for people you know well, and repent for ignoring His commission in the past. Repentance, not introspection and self-condemnation, is a good place to start in expanding your Kingdom experience. It increases your confidence before the Lord as you seek for breakthrough in any area of your life.

Familiarity is the culprit when we try to minister to those we know well. The people of Nazareth knew Jesus in the natural, asking, "Is this not Joseph's son?" Looking at Him merely as Joseph's son kept them from knowing Him as Savior and Lord, the way He intended. For that reason, Jesus did few miracles in His hometown (see Mark 6:1–6; Luke 4:22, NKJV).

When we pursue healing as the responsibility of every believer, we realize breakthroughs as we seek to serve those around us. This creates a momentum in the Spirit and increases our understanding of how God works in the miracle realm. This gives us greater confidence when we must deal with those closest to us who need a miracle.

Disappointment is inevitable for everyone pursuing this miracle lifestyle. It is also the biggest stumbling block for those who desperately want to see the ministry of Jesus restored to the Church. I had an interesting conversation recently with my friend Don Milam. He is an unusually well-read individual. He told me that when he studied the lives of many atheists and existentialists, he noticed that nearly every one of them believed for a miracle for a dying family member or friend but did not get it. Their coping mechanism became a belief system that got rid of the *"God is personal, powerful and at hand"* part of the equation.

I have seen pastors do this a lot. They become practical atheists, people who have a belief in God, but approach a problem the same way an atheist would—without a miracle-working God at the center of their answer. These leaders see something happen that they cannot explain and in response create a foolish doctrine or belief to take away the pressure of mystery. For example, when a child dies, they may say, "God took the life of this child because He needed another angel in heaven."

This statement may give temporary comfort to a grieving family, but it is a lie on several fronts. God does not turn the dead into angels, and He did not cause the death of that child. The lie brings temporary peace while undermining the parents' ability to truly be healed in their hearts, then rise up and seek the justice of the Lord in giving them vindication for their loss. There is a potential power in loss that gets lost itself in a cloud of disappointment. The lie also keeps them from pursuing a breakthrough anointing so that other parents do not have to feel the same grief and loss.

The fact that God can use tragedy has caused many to attribute tragedy to God. The simple solution is WWJD—*What would Jesus do?* He healed *all* who came to Him. His is the only standard worth pursuing.

Why did Jesus raise people from the dead? Because not everyone dies in God's timing. If we have the Father assigning people to die and Jesus raising them from the dead, we have a divided house. Those who believe that everything that happens is God's will are contributing to the perpetual immaturity of the Church. "The Lord is not slow about His promise, as some count slowness, but is patient toward you, *not wishing for any to perish* but for all to come to repentance" (2 Peter 3:9, emphasis added). It is not His will that any perish, but people perish every day in spite of it being against God's will.

Learning to live with the unexplainable is one of the most necessary ingredients of the Christian life, especially for those pursuing the authentic Gospel displayed through the miracle realm. If we do not give up our right to understand, we will seldom experience the peace that passes understanding that Philippians 4:7 talks about.

If everything worked perfectly for us the first time we tried, there would be little need for promises like, "And we know that God causes all things to work together for good to those who love God, to those who are called according to His purpose" (Romans 8:28). Verses like this are given to us because we are all *in process*. As Larry Randolph, a very gifted prophet and friend, stated, "God keeps all His promises. But He is not obligated to fulfill our potential." Much of what we have been contending for in recent years has to do with our potential made available through His Word.

Giants still must be slain in order for us to enter the land that Jesus promised us. I believe the biggest giant is disappointment. Everyone who pursues this ministry of the miraculous will face disappointment over and over again. That is why so many have opted for a lesser gospel. Without high expectations, you will seldom see this giant.

Look at Proverbs 13:12: "Hope deferred makes the heart sick, but desire fulfilled is a tree of life." One of the most spiritually vulnerable moments in a Christian's life is when loss or disappointment comes. It is as if our spiritual immune system breaks down, allowing disease of the heart to subtly pull us away from our moorings. "Has God said . . ." led Adam into eating the forbidden fruit.

It is normal for questions to arise during loss. Often these questions are important steps in development. The danger comes when these questions lead us away from God and His Word into human reasoning in conflict with God's Word. Whether we question what went wrong or if we did all that was necessary, this questioning usually leads us to wonder about God's promises and His goodness. To question the goodness of God is one of the most dangerous spiritual diseases. It comes on the heels of disappointment. We have to realize that this kind of situation must be redeemed by God's touch, or we will end up with the sick heart He warned about. It is a sick heart that no longer believes in the goodness of God.

The goodness of God is the cornerstone of our theology. When we start breaking down our concept of who God is, we are most vulnerable to the lies of the devil. Hope dissipates in direct proportion to our loss of understanding of God's goodness. Plus, lies never come without the accompaniment of the liar's personality. Believing a lie empowers the liar. And he comes "to steal and kill and destroy" (John 10:10). This is the number one reason Christians withdraw from a life of true biblical faith displaying the miraculous—because of our inability to deal with disappointment. It is much easier for some to just consider God angry and vindictive. That way we can explain our losses much more easily. But lies never satisfy the human spirit. It is only satisfied with truth that leads to His presence.

## Steps to Healing Our Hearts

Any disappointment that does not get touched redemptively by God will foul and fester, bringing infection into our souls. It slowly robs us of both emotional and intellectual strength, until the spirit is finally violated. My book *Strengthening Yourself in the Lord* (Destiny Image, 2007) deals with this subject much more thoroughly. But for now, here are some tools I use to enable healing in my heart:

*1. Be Honest with God*—Some people just need to weep before God in an honest baring of their souls. This kind of openness before the One *who never rejects us* is vital. Make sure to block out enough time for this process. Healing the heart in these seasons does not take place in a brief five-minute devotional. Take time. It is often a life-or-death issue in that your spiritual health is at risk.

It is important to approach God with confidence. "Therefore let us draw near with confidence to the throne of grace, so that we may receive mercy and find grace to help in time of need" (Hebrews 4:16). Get alone with God and cry out with honesty. I often pray something like this: *"Father, I know You are good and that You never lie or abandon Your children. But it sure feels and looks to me as if You did. It looks as if You didn't keep Your promise to me. I know my perception is wrong because You are always good. I need You to help me. Please heal my heart, and according to Your promises please deliver me quickly."*

Do not be religious. Do not say things you think God wants to hear. Bare your soul and be honest, but do not accuse Him in the name of honesty. I am not saying He will strike you down. I am just saying it is vital to never let these kinds of accusations enter your heart in the first place. If accusations dominate your thoughts, you have waited too long to come before Him in honesty. Quickly confess and repent.

*2. Listen to God*—I almost always go to the psalms for comfort. The psalms contain every emotion. They represent almost every conflict and tragedy we go through. I read until I hear my voice in the psalms and see my heart's cry. When I find this, I know I am close to an answer. At this point, it is important to meditate on His Word, where there is healing. Prayerfully review what He says over and over again. I will often take the words of a psalm and sing them, confess them and declare them. Sometimes I write out the words on a three-by-five card to carry with me, knowing the bigger issues take time for complete healing. I cannot afford to think differently about my situation than God does. Thinking differently is where I get into trouble.

When you do not take care of the issues of the heart, you paint a bull's-eye over yourself, giving the enemy an easy target. Proverbs 4:23 urges, "Watch over your heart with all *diligence*, for from it flow the springs of life" (emphasis added). The issues of life flow from this place within us. Keeping it clean, undefiled and intensely devoted has long-term benefits. This has been a priority verse for me over the last forty years.

*3. Receive the Peace*—Continue to go before God and pour out your heart until His peace starts to invade you. Keep in mind that if you do not give up the right to understand, you will not receive the peace that passes understanding. The healing you need does not start in the mind; it is not intellectual in nature. It targets the heart. It is in that place of recovering health that you are restored. In time, your understanding is renewed.

The one thing you do not want to do is devalue what God has taught you in the past. Look at it this way: You can only hold on to one thing at a time—the promise of God or disappointment. You will have to drop one to embrace the other.

*4. Feed Your Heart Correctly*—Feed your heart on what God is doing without stumbling over what He has not done or does not seem to be doing. I am not encouraging denial—your needs should be brought before God in the secret place (see Matthew 6:6). They are the needs that have not been met yet. Pray until you sense His heart on a matter. Agree with Him through decree. Then leave the burden in His presence, and live life by feeding on His faithfulness—what He *has* done. When the burden for the need becomes strong again, go back into the place of intimacy with God and let your voice be heard. My wife's book, *The Happy Intercessor* (Destiny Image, 2009), gives unusual insight into this approach to prayer.

Even John the Baptist struggled with the fact that disappointment distracts. He had already received a revelation that Jesus was the Lamb of God. But he began to question that insight while he was facing death in prison, so he sent two of his disciples to Jesus to find out the truth (see Matthew 11:2–3). How could the greatest of all Old Testament prophets question what he had learned? (The New Testament means *New Covenant*, which did not start until the blood was shed on the cross. John was the last of the Old Covenant Prophets; see Matthew 11:11.) I think John's attention was turned toward what God was *not* doing. He had prepared the way for the One who released people from prison (see Luke 4:18), yet he was in prison, about to die.

Jesus gave the wisest counsel possible: "Go and report to John what you hear and see" (Matthew 11:4). He directed John's attention to what God *was* doing. The climax of this lesson comes in Jesus' final statement to John's disciples: "And blessed is he who does not take offense at Me" (Matthew 11:6).

Dwelling on what God is not doing opens us up for the spirit of offense, which always leads to the ultimate sin of unbelief. That is ultimately a partnership with the demonic realm that seeks to undermine God's purposes in the earth, and worse yet, to bring the nature of God into question.

## Thankful and Hungry

We must cultivate two main attitudes as we pursue the miracle lifestyle Jesus assigned to us. The first attitude is thankfulness. I believe this is one of the most underrated expressions in life. It is vital that we offer sacrifices of thanksgiving to God for what we have seen and participated in. This attitude alone will help people who taste of success remain humble. Thanksgiving is an expression of true humility; it identifies God as the source for all that is good.

The second attitude we need is hunger. I must maintain a hunger for the more that God has promised. I am the most dangerous to myself, and to the movement I represent, when I take on the attitude of an expert. Sadly, by embracing that attitude, I have chosen where to level off in my growth. What I know can keep me from what I need to know if I don't remain a novice (childlike). A childlike approach to this miracle lifestyle will keep us honest, humble and continually growing.

Cultivating these two areas of the heart, thankfulness toward God and a hunger for more, will help maintain spiritual health, which in turn will affect every area of life. Be thankful. Stay hungry.

# 8

# THE POWER OF THE TESTIMONY

## *Bill*

O ne of the strongest influences in our healing culture comes from the value we place on the testimony. For us, the testimony is more than someone giving his or her story in a public setting. That is good and encourages us all. But there is a more deliberate way to live with this wonderful gift. Testimonies are to be preserved, rehearsed, kept honest and discussed in conversation. The stories of God's intervention set a legal precedent for the miraculous. They establish an understanding of His nature and His heart and provide the *ongoing* element to the miraculous.

Somewhere around 1980, I asked the Lord to give me understanding about a verse that stood out to me in my daily Scripture reading. I was reading Revelation 19, and verse 10 seemed to leap off the page: "For the testimony of Jesus is the spirit of prophecy." Something was happening in my heart over this verse, but I could not identify what it was, nor could I have taught on it if my life depended on it. Yet it was alive to me. It was obvious that the Holy Spirit was "hovering" over this verse and that there was something there for me. I asked Him to teach me what that phrase meant. (The principle I want to share from it is the concept *behind* the verse, not its primary focus.)

Later that same day, a man stopped by my office to tell me something. He was in such a rush that he would not even sit down. He just stood in my doorway and told me what God had done in his marriage. Before leaving, he said I could tell others about his experience. When he said I could share it with others, the same thing happened as when I read Revelation 19:10— my heart leapt. Except this time, I knew I had been given the beginning of an answer to my request for understanding.

The man left rather quickly and returned to work, so I turned to the Lord to process what had just happened. My friend had just told me about the healing of his marriage (testimony) and said I could share it with others (prophecy). Testimony and prophecy were the two main elements of the Scripture I had pondered over that morning. I could tell that the principle involved could profoundly impact how I conducted my life.

At the time, our church family was experiencing good worship, people were getting saved and broken lives were being mended. Testimonies seemed to encourage people by giving them hope that great things could happen to them, too. This was not a time when physical healings and miracles were taking place. That would come later. But I was on my way to discovering an important tool that would help us move forward into the miraculous.

## Understanding the Tool

As I studied the word *testimony* in the Old Testament, I found that it came from a word meaning "do again." That did it for me. I realized that God had hidden the miracle realm *for* us, not *from* us, in the mystery of the testimony. When He told Israel to keep the testimony, He was giving them something that would keep them in touch with His continual supernatural interventions.

The *testimony of Jesus* is a spoken or written record of anything Jesus has done. And the testimony of Jesus is the spirit of prophecy. Any time we share something that God has done in our lives, we release the spirit of prophecy. *Prophecy* comes in two main forms, one to foretell the future, and the other to release a word that changes the present. I believe the testimony of Jesus releases a prophetic anointing that has an effect on present realities. Things become possible in the present that were not available until the testimony was given. It is as though the testimony reveals what God wants to "do again."

Many often wonder if it is God's will for a miracle to happen. First of all, the Word declares that His will is to heal: "I am willing; be cleansed" (Mark 1:41). The Bible tells us that Jesus paid for our healing: "by whose stripes ye were healed" (1 Peter 2:24, KJV). But here are two stunning facts in this regard: "God is no respecter of persons," and "Jesus Christ is the same yesterday, today, and forever" (Acts 10:34, KJV; Hebrews 13:8, NKJV). That means what He has done for someone else, He would do for you (He is no respecter of persons), even if what He did happened a long time ago (He is the same yesterday, today, and forever). So testimonies reveal God's heart. They set a legal precedent for miracles.

While my journey toward understanding this area started in 1980, it was not until the late 1990s that I began to see the full impact of the testimony on both our present-day experience and our Kingdom culture. While speaking at a conference in Rochester, Minnesota, I ministered to a young lady who had been in a bad accident several years earlier. Her leg had been injured severely. She had pins holding her ankle together and had restricted movement and pain. She recovered some of the movement during prayer, and the pain lessened, as well.

When this lady got dressed for our meetings the next day, her husband looked at her leg and said, "Hey, that wasn't there before!" When she looked down, she noticed that the part of her calf muscle that had been missing had grown back overnight. She excitedly told me her story.

I got excited, too, and had her share her story with the attendees. We all praised God for this wonderful miracle. As she returned to her seat, another lady came up to me and said, "If God did that for her, certainly He would do that for me." I was impressed with her understanding of God's nature. She had also been in an accident, severing her Achilles tendon five years earlier. After it was reattached, part of the calf muscle failed to respond correctly and atrophied. She had to learn how to walk all over again. She wanted God to do the same kind of miracle for her.

I called the young lady who had already been healed back to the front and told her, "Freely you received, freely give" (Matthew 10:8). I asked her and the pastor's wife to lay hands on the lady with the Achilles injury. God created that missing/atrophied muscle right before their eyes. The lady could walk normally again. Excitement grew, and two other ladies came up who had had different kinds of accidents affecting the calf muscle. Both were instantly healed as God grew back the part of the muscle that was dwarfed in size.

I traveled from Minnesota to Tennessee for another conference. It brought great encouragement when I shared the stories of these four women. A medical doctor asked for prayer. He had broken his leg a year earlier and had restricted movement; his calf muscle had also atrophied. After our students had prayed over his leg for about twenty minutes, I asked him how he was doing. He told me the pain was gone and that movement was restored. I asked him specifically about his calf muscle. He told me he could feel the skin stretching.

Whenever I come home from a trip, I like to share the testimonies with our church family. The *spoil* is part of their reward for sending me out. When I told them the stories of these five people who had experienced a creative miracle in their legs, we had great rejoicing. Two weeks later, in another meeting at our church, a woman told me she had broken her leg a year earlier and that she had restricted movement and pain. The muscles in that leg had also atrophied from lack of use. She said that when I shared the testimony of the five miracles, her leg got hot, all the pain left, the movement was restored and the muscles grew back correctly. All this was the effect of the stories shared in an atmosphere of expectancy. The miracles from that one testimony continue.

We also had an amazing experience following the healing of a child with clubfeet. He was three years old at the time. One of his little friends came up to him afterward and said, "Run!" He took off running and came back to his friend and said, "I can run!" What an amazing miracle. The look on his face is one I will never forget. A few weeks later, neighbors of that child came to visit the church. When they introduced themselves as the child's neighbors, I asked how he was doing. They told me he had been running for the last two weeks!

Needless to say, that was a story we shared with the church family. Praise erupted from the crowd as the goodness of God was revealed once again. Miracles do that. (To withhold the lifestyle of miracles from the Church is to rob God of the glory that He is due.) Unknown to me, a family was visiting from out of state. They had a little girl about two years old whose feet turned inward so severely that she tripped over them when she tried to run. When the mother heard the story of the boy with clubfeet and also heard about the power of the testimony, she said in her heart, "I'll take that for my daughter." When the message was over, she went to our nursery to pick up her little girl. The girl's feet were already straight! No one had prayed. The miracle was released when the mother came into agreement with the report of the Lord.

## Keeping the Testimony

"You should diligently keep the commandments of the LORD your God, and His testimonies and His statutes which He has commanded you" (Deuteronomy 6:17). The word *keep* is interesting. It means "to watch" or "to preserve." It is translated in numerous ways, including "observe," "watchman" and "protect."

Growing up in Sunday school, I remember hearing often the importance of keeping God's commandments. Obedience can never be overrated. But I do not ever remember any instruction on keeping God's testimonies. Yet that is as much a part of Kingdom culture as is obedience. In fact, as we will see in a moment, the two are connected.

The instructions from Deuteronomy 6 address our responsibility with God's commandments, statutes and testimonies. Commandments show us how to live. Statutes show us how to think. Testimonies show us what to expect. A testimony reveals God's acts, which in turn reveal His ways. Each story contains wonderful revelation of God's nature and His heart for people.

Understanding God's way is the ultimate piece of information available to humanity. The testimony is therefore a priceless treasure. It is from an understanding of God's nature that Israel would be able to establish and sustain a Kingdom culture that would be blessed in every area of life. It is in this book of Moses that we receive the instruction to watch over and care for the priceless gift from heaven of the testimony. The mandates given in Deuteronomy 6 transcend the Old Testament law and become practical guidelines for sustaining spiritual health in a Christian culture. Our lifestyle, thought life and expectations have everything in the world to do with developing a culture that contains the ability to sustain a great move of God. Testimonies are a central piece to this puzzle.

In my staff meetings, I take anywhere from one to two hours every week just to share and review testimonies. We have chosen to feed ourselves on the works of God. It really makes a difference. I do something similar in our leadership prayer meeting and even our board meeting. We take time at the beginning to share the miracles. I cannot afford for us to make decisions based on human talent and resources. Faith lives from heaven toward earth. The testimony keeps us connected in thought to the God who knows no impossibilities.

I have even hired someone to record the stories of God's interventions. Pam sits in our staff meetings and records the reports that are given. She also interviews the people who are healed in our Healing Rooms ministry, and she does extensive work researching and recording the miracles that happen during a given week in our church life. Accuracy makes sure the testimony releases life. Embellishments undermine the very thing we intend. This is our effort to "keep" the testimony.

## The Testimony and Obedience

God has given us a treasure in each testimony. Each story is priceless and revelatory in that it speaks of the nature of God and His heart for people. The stories contain the record of His DNA. Treating these stories as wonderful gifts pleases Him. The testimony has a direct effect on the life of obedience, as seen in Psalm 78:9–11:

> The sons of Ephraim were archers equipped with
>   bows,
>   Yet they turned back in the day of battle.
> They did not keep the covenant of God
>   And refused to walk in His law;
> They forgot His deeds
>   And His miracles that He had shown them.

This psalm reveals cause and effect. Follow the digression of the sons of Ephraim: They were equipped and trained for battle, yet they turned back rather than risk all and fight. Why? Because they had not been walking in radical obedience. Failure at this point destroys all confidence in "the Lord fighting for us." Why did they not walk in obedience? They forgot the testimony—His deeds and miracles.

Conscious interaction with a personal, supernatural God brings about a complete change in a person's confidence level. I have watched this phenomenon for years. People who were once cowardly in their Christian life became bold disciples after seeing the Lord's miraculous ways. It is as though they went from being a member of a Christian club to being a soldier on the front battle lines. Awareness of God's ways has that effect on how people think and live. It happened for Israel. It happens today in the Church.

Tragically, I have also seen the opposite happen. I have watched those who were once passionate for God lose track of the God of the impossible and bury themselves in busy Christian activity void of the supernatural. And so the warriors become disarmed and powerless through the many activities that do nothing to increase the demonstration of God's power through love to those in need.

Keeping the testimony basically means that I diligently preserve the record of what God has done in the past until it becomes the lens through which I see present circumstances. Whenever I see circumstances through humanity's history with God, impossibilities turn into opportunities and tragic losses become occasions for Holy Spirit–inspired vindication.

Whenever Israel forgot God's works, they began to decline spiritually. As we continue to look at Psalm 78, we notice this theme in verses 40–43 (NKJV):

> How often they provoked Him in the wilderness,
>     And grieved Him in the desert!
> Yes, again and again they tempted God,
>     And limited the Holy One of Israel.
> They did not remember His power:
>     The day when He redeemed them from the enemy,
> When He worked His signs in Egypt,
>     And His wonders in the field of Zoan.

Israel brought great pain and disappointment to the Lord whenever they forgot His supernatural interventions. Somehow, maintaining awareness of His miraculous ways changed the way they lived. It became a reference point, something like the North Pole, in all their reasoning. This *supernatural* way of thinking should be sustained through conversation, song and instruction—all in an effort to keep the testimony.

When we forget the miracles, we talk about them less. When we talk about them less, we expect them even less. And if our expectations of the miraculous decline, miracles eventually disappear from our lives altogether. It is my personal conviction that every one of Israel's backslidings can be traced back to a time when they stopped keeping the testimony. Remaining conscious of the God who invades the impossible was supposed to keep them from the evils of idolatry and rebellion. Failure to keep the testimony removed the mental and emotional standard that protected them from becoming like other nations.

One of the most interesting parts of this truth about keeping the testimony is found in the story of Israel and the Tabernacle of Moses. God had given His people specific ways to do things, especially pertaining to worship. The single most important piece of furniture in the Tabernacle during the Temple era was the Ark of the Covenant. It was a box covered in gold that was placed inside the Holy of Holies. This is where the presence of God manifested for all of Israel. On the Day of Atonement, the high priest would come into this room that was lit only by the presence of the Lord. He was there to present the offering of blood to postpone the penalty of sin for one more year. No one else could enter, ever.

This Ark contained a jar of manna, the almond rod of Aaron and the tablets of stone with the Ten Commandments written on them. Since each of these items revealed the works of God, the Ark also became known as the Ark of the Testimony. On top of this golden box, two cherubim faced each other. Between those two angelic creatures was a seat for God called the mercy seat.

Here's a wonderful truth: Every time you share a testimony with someone, you usher the mercy seat of God into their lives. Each testimony gives an invitation for listeners to taste of God's mercy for themselves. This is part of the amazing purpose for the testimony in the Kingdom culture. It single-handedly sustains the miraculous, while at the same time inviting the uninitiated into a relationship with the One who alone can bring a redemptive touch to every single part of life.

## Strategic Prophecies

Whenever I visit another city or nation, I am often told about strongholds in the area. The host will inform me of the division in the church leadership and the hardness of heart toward the miraculous in the people of God. I can tell much research has gone into gathering this information. They continue by informing me of the cults active in the area and why revival has not come. I listen patiently, trying to feel their heart for their city. But I cannot be impressed with the devil's success or I will react to him. If I live in reaction to the powers of darkness, then the enemy has influenced how I set my agenda. Living in reaction to the devil is the counterfeit of living in response to the Lord. So I guard my heart from all such information.

A better approach would be for an area's leadership to recognize what kind of demonic influences are present, then look for one person who has been set free from such influence. For example, if your city is known for divorce, find someone who was near divorce but then experienced the healing grace of Jesus in their marriage. Have them give testimony of what God has done. Let the people of God arm themselves with stories that work against the spirit of the age. That spirit works to keep people hopeless in specific areas of their lives. Spreading testimonies through a city to counteract such hopelessness is hard at first, but soon it becomes the norm as people's expectations of what God can do increase exponentially.

The testimony of a healed marriage brings obvious encouragement to those who struggle in that area. But it is bigger than that. As we saw at the start of the chapter, Scripture says that the testimony of Jesus is the *spirit of prophecy*. The testimony of healed marriages prophesies God's intent for the whole city. This *spirit of prophecy* is an anointing that actually changes the atmosphere over a given location. When a big enough part of the Church boasts in God's redemptive work in marriages, a shift takes place in the atmosphere of a city such that people start thinking differently because the lies they assumed were true were dethroned. And that difference opens the door for true transformation.

Be forewarned, however. When you focus on an area that you want to see changed through the testimony, the enemy will target that area even more. He does not take kindly to our intention to take back lost territory. Yet do not fear. Intercessory prayer over a certain area will again turn the tide until the area of weakness actually becomes the area of greatest strength. Prayer for the marriages of the Church, for example, will make it so that God will broadcast the successes over a community to establish a new standard of marital success. All of this comes from the simple privilege of *keeping the testimony*.

# 9

# HEALING AND A PROSPEROUS SOUL

*Bill*

Healing is the great subject of this book. Learning how to be healed and how to get others healed is its intended focus. But the one thing greater than divine healing is divine health. Israel had it for a whole generation. They were in the wilderness, between Egypt and the Promised Land. It is amazing to me that the one generation to experience this blessing was in rebellion against God and not even born again. Since we live under a better covenant, it is important that we believe God for a fuller manifestation in this area than what we have seen to date. In Jeremiah 33:6, God said this about Jerusalem and its inhabitants: "Behold, I will bring to it health and healing, and I will heal them; and I will reveal to them an abundance of peace and truth." It is in the heart of God for His people to be blessed—spirit, soul and body.

While attending Genesis Bible Training Center in Santa Rosa, California, I was a janitor for a private firm, hired to clean many of the city and county office buildings. Night after night I cleaned offices, bathrooms and conference rooms. The place I found most fascinating was the police department. From the dispatch room to the offices to the squad rooms, I would see things that were far outside an average person's daily experience. One officer had two pictures under the glass top on his desk. One was a beautiful young lady, and the other was an older, sickly looking woman whom life had obviously abused. One day I noticed the note underneath these two pictures. It stated that they were the same woman, separated by only a few years. The difference was heroin. The effect of that deadly substance was obvious. This woman was truly among the walking dead.

Sin takes its toll on everything and everyone it touches. It is no secret that drug addiction and other serious sins affect our health. Medical professionals verify the destruction awaiting anyone who pursues such a careless lifestyle. We have all grieved as we have seen a large portion of our best and brightest destroyed by giving in to something they could not control. Sin destroys the health of a person's body, mind, emotions and spirit, brings devastation to a city and forever scars a family.

## Internal Realities

Many of our great doctors and psychologists have been focusing more and more on the possible connection between bodily sickness and internal issues like bitterness, anger, hatred and jealousy. We have heard for years that 85 percent of all sickness originates in the mind—not that it is imagined, just that it has its roots in an unhealthy thought life. While these internal issues are not injected into the arm or inhaled into the lungs, they poison the life of people who were created for significance. People's creative energies are redirected into the management of unhealthy thoughts and emotions, leaving them little or nothing for living in the purpose for which they were created.

For example, it is now fairly common knowledge even among secular counselors that people need to forgive others. If they do not forgive, it eventually eats away at their health. On many occasions, I have led a person into a prayer of repentance over unforgiveness, only to find that a miracle was *at hand* the whole time. But before the miracle manifested in his or her body, the person's heart also needed to be in agreement. I direct people to confess their sin specifically, not generally—meaning they need to tell God exactly whom they hold bitterness toward and confess that they no longer hold the person in judgment. I also have them pray a prayer of blessing over that person, if he or she is still alive.

I think that for believers, unforgiveness is the greatest cause of affliction. That ought not be the case. Scripture is plain on this subject: "But if you do not forgive others, then your Father will not forgive your transgressions" (Matthew 6:15). God in His mercy created the human body such that it is unable to live well in that environment. We must heed its signs.

Things like anxiety, regret, anger, hatred, unforgiveness and jealousy are known killers. They eat away at our immune systems and set us up for all kinds of physical calamities. Psalm 31:10 says, "For my life is spent with sorrow and my years with sighing; my strength has failed because of my iniquity, and my body has wasted away." The picture given in this verse is not hard to see. Sin destroys both emotional and physical strength, which opens the door for many physical problems. I can only imagine from eternity's perspective how surprised we will be at how many of life's problems were caused by, or at least aided by, a thought life inconsistent with the mind of Christ.

Isaiah 35:10 gives us an alternative to living with internal issues that promote poor health:

> And the ransomed of the LORD will return
> And come with joyful shouting to Zion,
> With everlasting joy upon their heads
> They will find gladness and joy,
> And sorrow and sighing will flee away.

*Ransomed* means "redeemed" or "purchased." Everyone who is born again has been redeemed—*purchased* by the blood of Jesus. Being *ransomed* is to have an effect on our internal world, where gladness and joy will chase away sorrow and sighing. What brought devastation in Psalm 31:10 is chased away by the joy of salvation in Isaiah 35:10. It may be challenging to live out, but it is not complicated.

## What the Body Reveals

I once prayed with a young lady for healing of Crohn's disease. This horrible affliction eats away at the colon, destroying all possibility of living a normal life. She had had that disease for seven years. In interviewing her before our prayer time, I asked her if she was hard on herself in the sense of being self-critical, judgmental and condemning. I was not accusing, and I made sure she understood that. It just came to mind, so I asked her in a nonthreatening way. She responded to my question with a yes.

Sometimes young people feel a lot of pressure to be great achievers. College students from certain cultures are especially guilty of this and put themselves under enormous pressure to make the grade. Missing their goal brings on all kinds of self-doubt, criticism and even self-inflicted punishment such as not eating, not sleeping properly or even worse.

I explained to this young woman that a colon eating itself is a physical manifestation of what she was doing to herself in her thoughts and in the heaviness she carried in her emotions. She had turned on herself with self-condemnation, and her body was simply manifesting on the outside what was happening on the inside. When I explained the connection, she saw it and was quite eager to repent. I led her in a prayer to confess the sin of self-abuse and renounce its effect on her life. Then I commanded the spirit of affliction to let go of her body. She instantly was healed.

It is crazy, but being critical and harsh toward ourselves can be as devastating as drug addiction. It is a slow burn I have seen over and over again. What is worse is that this kind of mindset is actually treated as a virtue by many in the church. Self-judgment and self-condemnation are even applauded as evidence that we are serious about following Jesus. At some point, we must believe that we are born again and must treat ourselves with the same respect we are commanded to show other believers.

The healed girl's mother wrote me a letter five months after I prayed with her daughter. She described her daughter's joy at Christmas. Around her were many gifts from her family, for which she was thankful. But what she wanted to talk about was her healing. She spoke about how five months earlier her life was over, but now she was well. She was now healthy on the inside and on the outside. Health was her portion. It had been God's will all along, but now she cooperated by directing her thought life to reflect His will. The emotions followed. When our mind follows His mind, our emotions are more likely to express His Kingdom with *peace and joy* (see Romans 14:17).

Confession is basically *agreeing with God*. Pretending that all is well, when it is not well, has no positive effect on our health. As Psalm 32:3 says, "When I kept silent about my sin, my body wasted away through my groaning all day long."

Secret sins devastate. They are like holding poison close to us until all in us is poisoned. Deep and complete confession is one of the most essential ingredients of a healthy lifestyle. Sometimes confessing to another believer who is mature and trustworthy can help provide the accountability we need to walk in success.

Jesus was perfectly healthy, but He had no sin. His forgiveness toward us gives us access to the same reality He enjoyed. But we must confess and truly believe His promise of forgiveness.

## A Rich Soul

There is an intrinsic connection between the health of a person's soul and his or her overall physical health. While I do not believe we should conclude that every disease is connected to some malady of the soul, I do believe our health is powerfully affected by how we think, what we feel and how we choose to live life. This realm called the *soul* calls the shots more often than we might imagine.

Consider 3 John 2: "Beloved, I pray that in all respects you may prosper and be in good health, *just as your soul prospers*" (emphasis added). When it says "just as your soul prospers," it means that in the same way as your internal world prospers and lives in blessing, so your external world should be blessed. If we could only give ourselves permission to live in the romance of loving God, and then learn to love ourselves properly, we would find out why the Bible commands us to love our neighbors by that standard. One reality paves the way for the other.

Most of us understand that our soul is comprised of our mind, emotions and will. What our will chooses has great impact on our thought life and on our emotional condition. Learning how to navigate this part of life is huge, affecting our health and even our finances. The verse we just looked at is fairly clear—prosperity is to touch every area of life, flowing from a healthy soul. This seems consistent with Proverbs 4:23: "Watch over your heart with all diligence, for from it flow the springs of life." Springs are to flow with life that touches every area.

There is no punishment in the mind of Christ. There is no self-hatred or frustration either. His mind is beautiful in every way. When our will reflects His, our emotions receive the best medicine possible. An alignment takes place that gives permission for the body to experience health. A healthy spirit makes for a healthy soul. A healthy soul makes it much more likely that we will enjoy physical health, too.

We were created to live healthy. Our bodies are designed to heal themselves. If I cut my finger, my body comes to attention, sending everything necessary to rebuild what was destroyed. But it must be understood that we were not designed to carry the weight of sins such as bitterness and unforgiveness. These do not fit into the category "My burden is light" that Jesus promised to those who follow Him (Matthew 11:30). Hidden sin has devastating effects.

One of the great mysteries of the Kingdom concerns how our internal world of thoughts, emotions and ambitions affects our external world of health and prosperity. Internal realities affect our external realities. In fact, in some ways they create an external reality. Jesus released peace in a storm, and the storm ceased. The peace was *in* Him before it was *around* Him. We see that phenomenon when He slept during that life-threatening storm. The peace He lived in positioned Him as the answer to the disciples' cry. He slept in the storm before the disciples were able to sleep in the boat.

Because of what was in Him, whenever Jesus talked, a shift took place in the atmosphere around Him. The people around Him did not know what was happening; all they knew was that He spoke "as one having authority" (Matthew 7:29). Yet Jesus informed them that spirit and life were released through His words (see John 6:63). Peter demonstrated this phenomenon later. Because of the Spirit in him, when he walked to the Temple to pray, those in his shadow were healed. We, too, are carriers of the divine. It is released in the atmosphere of faith in His abiding presence.

Sickness entered the world when sin did. Sickness is to my body what sin is to my soul. Psalm 31:9 connects them: "Be gracious to me, O LORD, for I am in distress; My eye is wasted away from grief, my soul and my body also." Sin and sickness are also both dealt with by the same redemptive touch. Often they are spoken of in the same breath. Here are only a few of the many examples in Scripture:

> Which is easier, to say, "Your sins are forgiven," or to say, "Get up, and walk"?
>
> Matthew 9:5

> Who pardons all your iniquities,
> Who heals all your diseases.
> Psalm 103:3

> And no resident will say, "I am sick";
> The people who dwell there will be forgiven their iniquity.
> Isaiah 33:24

180

Is anyone among you sick? Then he must call for the elders of the church and they are to pray over him, anointing him with oil in the name of the Lord; and the prayer offered in faith will restore the one who is sick, and the Lord will raise him up, and if he has committed sins, they will be forgiven him.

James 5:14–15

But He was wounded for our transgressions, He was bruised for our guilt and iniquities; the chastisement [needful to obtain] peace and well-being for us was upon Him, and with the stripes [that wounded] Him we are healed and made whole.

Isaiah 53:5, AMP

## From Red to Black

It is fairly clear that sin causes problems that include physical sickness and disease. But the goal should not be simply to deal with the negative effects on our lives. That is like getting out of the red financially. If I do not get into the black, I still have nothing. The mind of Christ takes us into the black until we become whole, having the ability to contribute to society and bring about transformation. God meant for us to experience more.

God's intended realm of health is more than being able to get healed. It involves a realm of mental and emotional health that was seen clearly in the person of Jesus. He lived without regret, hatred, selfish ambition, greed, unforgiveness, anxiety, shame or guilt. He lived with the ability to bring a heavenly answer to every earthly problem. He spoke, changing the atmosphere and reality that surrounded the hearer. His miracles spoke of His nature and His intentions for the earth. He is still the Creator, carrying the perfect sense of purpose for every situation, knowing that heaven indeed must come to earth. He brokered another realm, another world into this one. He provided an example that went beyond avoiding sin. He revealed purpose and destiny. He revealed the unlimited resources available to anyone who would embrace this assignment. Jesus alone illustrated life in the black as His great purpose was to reveal the Father, the source of all these things.

It would be horribly wrong for me to even suggest that anyone who is sick has hidden sin in their lives. I do not believe that for a moment. But it would be equally wrong for me to ignore the connection of these two subjects in Scripture: a healthy soul and physical health. They are linked in kind. The biblical solution, at least in part, is to deal with the soul of the believer. For example, many would experience healing if they would just forgive others. Some would experience their miracle if they just believed they were actually forgiven by God and followed suit by forgiving themselves accordingly. These are real solutions for real situations.

Often, we reject asking people questions about the deep issues of the soul for fear of causing them pain. While concern for the feelings of others is to be applauded, we must not be so concerned about avoiding discomfort that we fail to reach a greater understanding of how their physical health is related to their souls. We must address this without accusing the sick of being in sin or being weak in character. We also must not wait for science to figure it out for us. The answers are in the owner's manual—the Bible.

## Real Wealth

I have a wonderful wife who has loved me faithfully now for thirty-eight years. I have three amazing children, all of whom are married to champions in their own right. They love me and are devoted to me as their dad, both natural and spiritual. From these three families we have nine grandchildren, who think I am wonderful. I do not know how I could become any richer. I guess there is always room for more money, but true wealth is not measured in bank accounts. It is measured in family, favor with God and man, and the ability to live with a fullness of purpose. That is true wealth. When the soul is healthy, all these things get added to our lives in one form or another. This is the "prosper in all things" spoken of in 3 John 2.

I believe God wants each believer to prosper. I also live with the painful awareness of how few believers can handle the blessing of the Lord. Israel had continual issues with surviving the blessings of God. Some believers also seem suspicious of the blessed life, having come to the conclusion that persecution and opposition are the only circumstances in which the Church thrives. The grace of God makes it possible to face such circumstances, yet God also gave instruction on how to live a peaceable life with leaders, authorities and governments (see 1 Timothy 2:1–2). There is room for a life of health and peace—that is His will.

Can we live with blessing and actually increase in spirituality? Yes! We must learn this since one of the last-days revelations of God will be centered on His goodness (see Jeremiah 33:9; Hosea 3:5). If we focus on the purpose of blessing, we can navigate well in this next season where God actually releases blessing on His people equal to the health of their souls. It is prosperity with purpose. If I am empowered with blessed relationships, finances, favor with governments or any other area of prosperity you can think of, it can be used for the glory of God. It must be used to promote the Kingdom.

To live prosperously in the blessings of God, it is vitally important to be free of bondage. Understanding the nature of bondage, whether it is sickness or torment, will help us learn how to dismantle its influence. When He announced His ministry, Jesus addressed bondage by revealing its nature:

> The Spirit of the LORD God is upon me,
> Because the LORD has anointed me
> To bring good news to the afflicted;
> He has sent me to bind up the brokenhearted,
> To proclaim liberty to *captives*
> And freedom to *prisoners*.
>
> Isaiah 61:1, emphasis added

Jesus said He will set both prisoners and captives free. Prisoners are behind bars because of what they have done. Captives are imprisoned because of what has been done to them. The key for the prisoner is to repent and be forgiven. Much release comes to those who truly, deeply repent. But the captive faces a different challenge altogether. Sometimes captives need to forgive others; sometimes they just need to use the authority given them to get out of captivity. Paul and Silas praised God in prison and the doors opened (see Acts 16:25–34). Praising God before a breakthrough comes has to be one of the greatest signs of a prosperous soul.

## Moving into Health

I do not get too excited about books that provide Christian formulas as the key to getting answers from God. They tend to rob readers of the privilege of pursuing and encountering God for themselves. When we pursue God for ourselves, we discover His unique plan for our situation.

Having said that, however, I do want to provide some principles here related to the subject of a prosperous soul. These will help us at least make a solid beginning. From there, as you encounter God for yourself, He will show you more and more. But please remember, this subject of moving into health with a prosperous soul is worthy of volumes. A small chapter in a book could never contain all that God intends for us in this area.

### Praise

Scripture exhorts us to give God thanks in every situation (see 1 Thessalonians 5:18). Israel was to send Judah first into battle (see Judges 1:1–2). *Judah* means "praise." God inhabits praise. Time in God's manifested presence changes us more than we could possibly imagine. It is key to the prosperity of the soul:

> Therefore they shall come and sing in the height of
> Zion,
> Streaming to the goodness of the LORD—
> For wheat and new wine and oil,
> For the young of the flock and the herd;
> Their souls shall be like a well-watered garden,
> And they shall sorrow no more at all.
> "Then shall the virgin rejoice in the dance,
> And the young men and the old, together;
> For I will turn their mourning to joy,
> Will comfort them,
> And make them rejoice rather than sorrow.
> I will satiate the soul of the priests with
> abundance,
> And My people shall be satisfied with My goodness, says the LORD."
> Jeremiah 31:12–14, NKJV

This is an amazing promise of God available for each one of us—that our souls would be like a well-watered garden. This is the Old Testament equivalent of 3 John 2. Prosperity of soul is seen in joy, rejoicing, comfort from His presence and an overwhelming abundance of God. This is His heart.

The final verse in this passage reveals a secret. It is the priests who have a satiated soul. *Satiate* means to "overeat immodestly." The picture is of one who is gorged beyond being full. This is the picture of the priest. The priest is one who ministers to the Lord in thanksgiving, praise and worship. A satiated soul is the result of the overwhelming presence of God upon those who offer themselves as a living sacrifice for His glory. Abundance that goes beyond measure is what turns the human soul into the instrument God intended, designed to reflect His extreme generosity!

### Biblical Meditation

Mankind is to live from every word that comes from the mouth of God. Every word gives life. We are sometimes guilty of reading the Scriptures as though they were merely a book to study, or worse yet, a contract to learn about. They are from an intimate One who wrote with our eternal purpose in mind. They are a love letter to be consumed out of passion for the One who breathed life into us, not merely a text to memorize.

> My son, give attention to my words;
>    Incline your ear to my sayings.
>    Do not let them depart from your eyes;
>    Keep them in the midst of your heart;
>    For they *are* life to those who find them,
>    And health to all their flesh.
>                    Proverbs 4:20–22, NKJV

The Bible is filled with this kind of instruction. But I doubt we need any verse other than this. We are to keep the things He says before our eyes in order to keep them in our hearts, so they will bring life to every part of our lives. This becomes evident in the area of physical health.

Isaiah 26:3 says, "The steadfast of mind You will keep in perfect peace, because he trusts in You." *Peace* is one of the most wonderful words in the Bible. It is a word that means wholeness, soundness of mind, health and prosperity. It is what 3 John 2 spoke of—it is the prosperous soul. The one who keeps his or her focus on God is filled with *peace*. I believe that in part, this refers to the art of biblical meditation, which seems to be a missing tool in today's army of believers. Biblical meditation is quieting the heart and reviewing what God has said over and over again until it becomes a part of us. It is a continuous review of the Word of the Lord, until that Word sinks in deeper than all other ideas and thoughts raised up against the knowledge of God. The prosperity of our souls has a definite connection to our response to God's Word.

### Good Works

Many of us have caught a glimpse of what God is doing in raising up believers to high places of influence. While I get excited over this prospect, it also concerns me. Our strong suit is not ruling. It is serving.

If we could somehow learn to rule with the heart of a servant and serve with the heart of a king, I think we could make this next transition victoriously. Just as God gives prosperity with a purpose, so He gives promotion with a purpose. Favored people are to empower others to succeed. It is that simple. Kings in God's Kingdom do not rule to build personal empires. They rule so that the citizens in their kingdom fulfill their purpose in life and discover the capacity to dream under their leadership. This is a biblical king. And while we have many different stations in life, we are kings and priests before God (see Revelation 1:6, NKJV). As kings, we represent His Kingdom and His rulership to touch people with His favor.

*Good works* is actually one of the three sacrifices mentioned in Hebrews 13:15–16. The other two are praise and fellowship. The Scriptures on this subject are many. But the best example is found in the servant of all, Jesus Christ (see John 13:3–8). He washed His disciples' feet, and yet He was said to have more joy than anyone else around Him (see Hebrews 1:9). He is the ultimate example of a prosperous soul.

Many would experience healing if they would just serve someone else. Sickness sometimes attracts attention that is not good for us. It is important to realize that giving honor to others releases life. Serving others positions us for rarely discovered joy. This is the way to a prosperous soul. As a bonus, I have seen numerous times when people who are praying for someone else's healing get healed themselves in the process.

## The Happy Soul

Cain offered a sacrifice that was unacceptable to God. His brother offered one that pleased God. Cain became jealous and contemplated murder. God's word of warning to him is quite revealing: "If you do well, will not your countenance be lifted up? And if you do not do well, sin is crouching at the door; and its desire is for you, but you must master it" (Genesis 4:7).

Sin is crouching at the door, but it can be beaten. *Doing well* is the answer. It is a phrase that basically means "to prosper, be glad." It also means "pleasing." If Cain would have discovered the prosperity of soul available through honoring his brother, sin would have lost its grip on his heart.

God designed us for joy. He created us to have more wealth in our souls than the greatest billionaire of our day has money in the bank. And it is from that great storehouse we get to live and help others come into their destiny in God. This is the privilege of a believer—to give out of overflow, out of a prosperous soul.

# 10

## WORDS OF KNOWLEDGE
## FOR HEALING

*Randy*

Several years ago, I was preparing to minister at a large conference. My youngest son, Jeremiah, who was about twelve at the time, came up to me and said, "What are you doing, Dad?"

I answered, "I'm getting words of knowledge for later, when I minister."

He then asked, "How do you get them?"

I told him, "Usually I feel them, maybe by feeling a pain that isn't mine. Sometimes they come as impressions. Sometimes I see them like a mental picture or a daydream." I did not tell him all the ways, just the most common.

Jeremiah stood there a few minutes and then said, "I'm getting one, Dad."

I asked him what it was. He told me, and I wrote it down with mine. (I cannot remember past about five words before I start forgetting some of them.) Jeremiah continued to stand there, and over several minutes he told me half a dozen more words of knowledge.

I wrote them all down and told him, "I've written your words down along with mine. Mine are on this side of the paper, and yours are on the other side. I'm about to go to the platform and give these words of knowledge and pray for healing. Would you want to come help me? I'll give my words and pray for healing, and then you give your words and pray for healing."

"Okay," he said. He gave me another word and then added, "Don't write that one down—that's my pain."

I was impressed. He knew instinctively not to list his own pains as words of knowledge. And later Jeremiah displayed neither fear of man nor stage freight. He stood before twelve hundred people, gave his words and prayed for people to be healed. And they were!

I believe that you, too, will begin receiving words of knowledge once I explain how to recognize them. Let me tell you how I began teaching and activating people in this gift. After my first experience of giving a word of knowledge in my local church, I was both very excited and very concerned. I thought, *I'm the only person in my whole church who knows how to recognize a word of knowledge. So if God wants to give a word for someone, it will have to come through me. That's a lot of pressure! But if I teach my church how to recognize words of knowledge, then everyone will be a candidate for God to use. That would take the pressure off me.*

That Sunday evening, I taught on words of knowledge for the first time. I had only had one myself and had no illustrations. We sang a song, I taught on words of knowledge and then we went back into worship. This was followed by a testimony time where people could stand and testify to God's goodness in their lives.

During testimony time, a lady who was a new convert stood up and said, "I think I'm a havin' one of them there things you've been talkin' about. My left wrist is a-killin' me, and there ain't nothin' wrong with my left wrist."

I waited, but no one stood with a wrist problem. Then the lady sat down. I thought she had missed it and felt sorry for her. Then just before the benediction, another woman stood up crying. "My wrists are in terrible shape," she said. "I've already had surgery and had plastic pieces put in them. I can't do my work, and I'm facing another surgery."

We prayed for her, anointing her with oil. I had everyone in the church come and pray by laying hands on her. If they could not touch her, they were to lay hands on the person in front of them, who was laying hands on her. She was totally healed. Twenty-six years later, she has maintained her healing.

This was the second time in two weeks that someone was healed at church through words of knowledge. God was with us in our innocence. We did not know what we were doing, but we were determined to learn how to pray for the sick more effectively.

I first started teaching on the activation of words of knowledge not because I wanted to be faithful to Ephesians 4:11–12, "It was he who gave some to be apostles, some to be prophets, some to be evangelists, and some to be pastors and teachers, to prepare God's people for works of service, so that the body of Christ may be built up." It was also not because I was altruistic or because I was aware of a prophecy that I was to do this. No—I began out of fear of having all the pressure on me. But regardless of the reason I started, I have since found that every time I teach on this subject, the gift is activated and/or imparted to one or more persons, and they begin to move in the gift immediately following the teaching. That had happened with my son Jeremiah when I taught him about the gift, and it usually happens with at least 10 percent of a congregation when I teach.

## Three Ways to Receive

One story illustrates three of the ways of receiving words of knowledge—by feeling, by seeing and by thinking. These are not the only ways to receive, as you will see, but they are some of the most frequent ways. I was in Birmingham, Alabama, praying for the sick and using words of knowledge to build faith. I felt a pain in my lower back. I counted my vertebrae and believed it was the third disc/vertebrae that needed healing. I gave the word of knowledge "Someone here has a problem in their third disc/vertebrae area."

No one responded.

Then I had an impression and gave it: "It's a man."

Still no one responded.

Then I saw a mental picture of a man tripping over a green hose. I said, "You were hurt by tripping over a green garden hose."

Still no one responded.

My back continued to hurt, and the impressions continued. Several more times I gave the word. I also gave other words, and people responded to those and were healed. Finally I said, "I don't get it. I *know* someone has this problem. Would you please identify yourself?"

A man stood up and said, "I have a problem with my third lumbar disc. I almost stood up earlier because I tripped over a green hose, but it wasn't a garden hose, it was a green aeronautical hose. I work at the airport."

I then realized I had allowed my interpretation of the hose to contaminate the word of knowledge. The only green hose I had ever seen was a green garden hose. God had not told me it was a garden hose specifically. That was my interpretation, and it had taken away the man's faith since it was not a garden hose he had tripped over.

I apologized, "I'm sorry! God didn't tell me it was a garden hose. I added that because it's the only kind of green hose I've ever seen."

We prayed for the man, and he was healed.

This word of knowledge was a combination of multiple words that came in multiple ways. First, I felt it in my own back. Second, by means of an impression, the thought came that it was a man. Third, I saw a mental picture of him tripping over a green hose. Together it was one word of knowledge with three pieces of information.

The lesson is this: Be alert for the different ways a word can come, and when it does come, be as specific as you can about it. The more specific you are, the more faith the word of knowledge creates—but be careful *not* to interject into the word of knowledge information that is from you rather than God.

Some other stories may help you get a better idea of how you can apply this lesson. When we first began to minister healing and words of knowledge, my wife received a word that resulted in a ten-year-old girl being healed of a rare kidney disease. On the way home from the meeting, I asked DeAnne how she had received this word of knowledge.

"I saw it," she said.

I then asked, "How did you know it was a kidney? You don't know anything about human anatomy."

She responded, "I didn't know what it was, so I asked, 'God, what's that?' He told me it was a kidney."

This came as an impression, not an audible voice, and DeAnne received more information by asking God to clarify it.

One time I was doing an activation clinic at Bill Johnson's church for those who had never had a word of knowledge. I invited them to come forward and give their first word. A woman came and said, "Water bottle." That's what she saw.

I said, "I don't know how to interpret that word. Does it make sense to anyone?"

Another woman was instantly healed by the word. She had no saliva glands and had to carry a water bottle with her all the time. She knew it was a word for her, and it created the faith that brought the healing.

On a trip to Brazil, a man gave the word "White Stallion" as what he had seen. This led to a woman being healed of many conditions. She had been riding a white stallion that had reared up and fallen over on her, then rolled over her. She knew this word was for her; it created faith and she was instantly healed.

Another time, I was in Odessa, Ukraine, teaching at a Messianic Jewish congregation. I saw a split-second mental picture of a couple girls walking alongside a road. A tractor came around the curve, pulling a sickle that cuts grass to make hay. The blade had fallen down without the driver realizing it. When he passed the girls, the blade almost cut off one girl's legs at the knees. I thought, *This is a crazy word to give in a city. If I were on a collective farm, it would make more sense.* But I gave it anyway.

Immediately a woman in her sixties stood up. She was the girl, and her injury happened exactly as I had described it. Her tendons and nerves had been severed, and she almost lost her legs. All these years, she could not bend her knees and was not able to walk up stairs unless she turned backward and swung her legs, which could not bend to the next step. She was instantly and totally healed.

Earlier, I related the story of my associate pastor, Tom Simpson, who saw an open vision three times in one day that resulted in a twelve-year-old boy being healed of a potentially terminal illness. Tom could not see anything but the vision. This was not a mental picture like a daydream; it was like watching a movie. Tom and I each received a visual word, but note the difference between them. Tom's was more of an open vision that occupied his entire field of vision, with everything else disappearing from view. Mine was more of an internal mental picture, a split-second, fleeting visual like a daydream. Visual words can come either way.

One of the most gifted early leaders in the Vineyard movement was Blaine Cook. He told me that once in a vision he saw a file folder open up with a person's medical chart inside. He actually read the conditions the person had. He did not know what some of the conditions were, but he could read them off the chart.

Once while ministering to my daughter's friend, I asked her about a name as I was praying. I asked if this name meant anything to her. She responded that it did not. Later she told me she had lied. The name was her biological father's pet name for her. A divorce had taken place when she was very young, and she had been adopted by her stepfather. She told me that she was not ready to deal with the emotions involved in this situation and had therefore lied, but she knew the name was from God. I just heard myself say the name without thinking about it. This is an example of words of knowledge coming as automatic speech.

Another time, I was illustrating what a word of knowledge is and how such words build faith. I walked down into the crowd, went up to someone randomly and said, "If Jesus came and stood in front of you and told you, 'You have a problem with migraine headaches' and wanted to heal you, how would that make you feel?"

The person started crying instantly. I realized that what I thought was a random pick for a random illustration had actually been a word of knowledge. I said to the woman, "You actually have migraines, don't you?"

She nodded her head yes. I prayed for her, and she was healed.

Later in another city, I used the same "random" teaching illustration in the same way. The random person I chose also began to cry. I stopped and said, "You have this condition, don't you?"

She responded that she did. These were not accidents or coincidences. Instead, they were so subtle that I was unaware that I was actually hearing from God for the person I was choosing.

## Dreams and Unusual Experiences

While ministering to leaders in Mozambique who were part of Rolland and Heidi Baker's ministry, I had the opportunity to interview three pastors who had each raised more than one person from the dead. After the interview, I asked them how they received words of knowledge. They told me they dreamed almost all of their words of knowledge.

Shortly afterward, I was in Brazil and had a dream. I clearly saw two hands with long splinters stuck into them from the bottom of the index finger around the thumb area and then to the center of the palms. The splinters came all the way out two inches past the other side of the hand. I was not sure this was God, never having received a word in a dream. In a meeting, I gave the word last in case I was wrong. A man seated on the back row quickly came to the front. He put his outstretched hand in mine. Before I could pray a sentence he was healed. I could see the large scar exactly as I had described it. He had been in pain since the accident, and his hand had been paralyzed in an open position. The pain and the paralysis ended a few seconds after he laid his hand in mine. (I am not sure why I saw two hands in the dream, whereas the man had injured only one. I was just glad to receive a word of knowledge that brought about his healing.)

That night one of my interns, Annie, also had a dream. She saw a large box fall on a man and heard three pops. The next day in a different city, a man entered her line for healing. She was not confident enough to give the dream as a word of knowledge. When the man told her his back had been broken in three places and fractured in fourteen due to a large wooden box falling on him at work, her faith was encouraged and she told him about the dream. His faith was encouraged, too, and he was healed of the pain he had experienced going down his legs since his surgery. He also suffered major constriction of his neck movement, but that, too, was healed. Full movement in both his neck and legs was restored.

In Uberlandia, Brazil, a woman told me she had dreamed she was receiving change from a woman. The woman in the dream told her, "When your friend who is in need of healing meets the man whose name is on the other side of this coin, she will be healed." When she turned the coin over, it had my name on it, then the dream ended.

Later, this woman traveled through a nearby city and saw a poster with my name on it advertising a healing meeting. She brought her friend, who was close to dying from cancer throughout her abdomen and in her femur bones. My faith was so encouraged by her story of the dream that I knew her friend would be healed. We prayed for almost twenty minutes before there was any sign of the presence of God healing her. Then the power of God came on her and continued for over an hour and a half, and she was healed of her cancer.

Unusual experiences are another way to receive words of knowledge. In an unusual phone occurrence, one time my wife could not get people off our private phone line. They were having an adulterous conversation. She tried over and over to get them off by hanging up and picking up again. Nothing worked. A few days later, on Sunday, the Lord reminded her of this experience and interpreted it to her. She gave a word that someone in our church was about to fall into sin via phone conversations, which were leading up to the adultery. A man came forward after church and confessed he was the man.

## Growing in Discernment

Sometimes getting words of knowledge can be confusing. They come in various ways at various times for various people. By trial and error, you can develop greater discernment in how to interpret words of knowledge. You may receive several words close together, for example, and you may not be sure if they are for several people or for just one person. Until your discernment develops, it is good to say, "I am not sure if these words are for one person or for different individuals."

Prior to preaching in Bishop Joseph Garlington's church in Pittsburgh once, I had been telling the Lord I needed to grow in impressions as a means of receiving words of knowledge. When I first started recognizing words of knowledge I was 32. I did not usually have any bodily pains. If I felt pain as a means of getting a word, I was about 95 percent accurate. If I had an impression, I was only about 25 percent accurate. Instead of growing in the area of impressions, I would not go for them and would only give words I felt by means of a pain. Twenty years later, however, I realize my own bodily pains as I age could cause my accuracy in that area to decrease. So I began praying, "Lord, I need to grow in impressions and other ways of recognizing words of knowledge. Give me impressions."

At Bishop Garlington's church, I felt a pain in my back and had an impression that it was from an accident. This was followed by a split-second mental picture of what I thought was a green Jeep Cherokee. I was not sure this was God, so when I gave the word I said, "I think someone here has injured his or her back in an accident." I did not say by driving a green Jeep Cherokee because I was too afraid it was not really a word of knowledge. But I had written it down on paper in my Bible.

A man stood up and said, "That's my daughter. She was hurt in her green Jeep Cherokee."

I was excited that I had heard correctly, yet disappointed that I had not given the full word. To increase the man's faith, I came down off the platform and showed him my note about the green Jeep Cherokee. Because I was so concerned about accuracy, I played it too safe and did not say what I thought I had seen.

This illustrates the process of receiving information by means of often very subtle impressions or mental pictures and how hard it is at first to know if it is God or not. It would have been better for me to have said, "And I think the person might have been driving a green Jeep Cherokee, but I am not sure."

Another time, I misinterpreted information from the Lord. I felt a pain in the neck and asked the Lord which vertebra.

I then had the impression that it was the sixth, which made sense in regard to the pain's location. I gave the word, then I had the impression it was a woman. I gave that word as well. Then I had the impression there were three women with this problem, so I added that word. Finally I had the strong impression "52." So I said, "And you are 52 years old."

No one came forward during the ministry time for this particular word, yet it was the strongest I had received. However, after the ministry time a woman came up to me and said, "Everything you said was true and accurate for me, but I am not 52, I am 57. I was born in 1952."

While she was telling me this, two other women came up with the exact same story. I had interpreted "52" as an age, when I should have said, "I am hearing the number 52—does that mean anything to the three women with the pain in their sixth cervical vertebrae?"

I hope you can learn as much from these stories of how I missed it as you can from the stories of how I got it right! Learning how to know what the Father is doing, saying and revealing is more an art than a science. And once you begin recognizing and receiving words of knowledge, then there is the matter of knowing how to give them once you get them.

## Giving Words of Knowledge

Let me briefly address how to give words of knowledge. When you begin, you will need time to develop your discernment. You need to determine when it is you and when it is the Holy Spirit. Give your words of knowledge humbly. Model humility. Never talk as if you are sure when you are not. Be honest. Use phrases such as, "I think someone might have . . ."

When words of knowledge involve healing relationships or emotions or lifting burdens, sometimes they can be quite sensitive. I say in such cases, "I don't know you. I'm having an impression. I'm trying to learn how to hear from God. If what I say bears witness in your heart that it is true, receive it, but if it doesn't, let it be like water on a duck's back—don't receive it. In that case, I am missing God."

On the other hand, if you are certain, do not pretend you are not. Be authentic, honest and genuine. Be humble enough to admit it when you miss. Also, be natural in the supernatural. Do not change the way you talk or become spooky spiritual. It is important that we learn to move in the supernatural naturally, without hype, manipulation, suggestion or in ways that would not work outside the church setting in the secular arena. We want the gifts to be modeled in such a way that people take them into their daily secular jobs and activities.

It is not only important to know how to receive words and give them, it is also important to understand their significant relationship to the gifts of healing. In 1 Corinthians 12 both "words of knowledge" and "gifts of healings" are mentioned (see verses 7–11, NKJV). These two go together. Though words of knowledge are not just for healing, they play a major role in healing. It is as if the two were married, just as tongues and interpretation are married, discerning of spirits and prophecy are married and gifts of faith and the working of miracles are married. (With the word of wisdom being complementary to all the gifts.)

I usually use the following two illustrations when I am about to minister in words of knowledge. In Mark 10, blind Bartimaeus desperately cried out for Jesus to have mercy on him. Stopping, Jesus said, "Call him." So the disciples told Bartimaeus, "Cheer up! On your feet! He's calling you" (verse 49).

This gave Bartimaeus great faith, which he indicated by throwing his cloak to the ground. This cloak was like his social security disability card. It was given by the religious establishment to indicate he was a legitimate beggar, not a scam artist. In his heart, he knew he would not need it anymore. What caused this kind of faith? Hearing the words, "He's calling you!"

That is a word of knowledge. Jesus, through His disciples, shares who and what He wants to heal. I often pick out someone on the first row and ask them, "How would you feel if Jesus appeared, stood in front of you and said, 'I want to heal you tonight'? Would you be excited? Why? Would you be certain you would be healed? Why?"

They usually say, "Because Jesus said so." That generates excitement. People are certain they would be healed if Jesus told them He wanted to heal them. That is exactly what He does in a word of knowledge. When people truly understand the purpose of such words and are the benefactors of one (meaning they are the one about whom the word is given), it creates an excitement and a confidence that they will indeed be healed—because Jesus said so through the word of knowledge.

The late Omar Cabrera, a famous healing evangelist in Argentina, once told me how important it is to make sure people understand the purpose of words of knowledge. He told me that if they do not, words only create curiosity, but if they do, words create faith. I have found this is true. Over a decade ago, I went to Argentina and ministered for Omar Cabrera in six cities. In one city, I gave instructions, as usual, for people to respond by waving their hands when they were 80 percent healed or more. I gave a word of knowledge, and a quarter of the people who stood up in response were waving their hands over their heads immediately. I told my interpreter to tell them not to wave when they were *believing* for their healing, but to wait until it manifested at least 80 percent in their bodies first. I gave another word and the same thing happened, so I told the interpreter the same thing. This occurred twice more. The last time, I told him, "They don't understand!"

My interpreter replied, "*They* do understand—you're the one who doesn't understand. These churches were built on healings related to words of knowledge. Why are you thinking that you have to pray before they can be healed? The word of knowledge creates the faith that heals them. Many are healed before you ever pray in Omar's churches."

I was so excited when I heard that. Back in America, I shared my experience and began to see people healed in America, too, before I prayed for healing. What had changed? Was disease any weaker than before, or was God any stronger? No. The only thing that had changed was my expectation and understanding of how people could be healed by a word of knowledge and the faith it built before prayer.

## Words as Numbers or Indicators

Sometimes a word of knowledge identifies the condition that needs healing. One time, I heard the number "9" and gave it in a large meeting where we were praying for people with metal in their bodies. I said, "I am hearing '9,' but I don't know what it means."

A man came up later who had been healed of immobility caused by all his vertebrae being fused from the tailbone to the eleventh thoracic vertebra. He had 9 screws in his back, yet now he could move his legs in ways he had not been able to since before his 5 surgeries. He could also bend over, touch his toes and move his arms back without pinching his back.

Sometimes words of knowledge that come as numbers have multiple fulfillments. I gave the number "7" a couple nights before I wrote this. A woman was healed of her neck problem in her seventh vertebrae. Another woman's problem began 7 years ago with an unsuccessful surgery. And two others whose problem was connected with the number 7 were also healed.

Other times, numbers will have meanings you could never have interpreted. They can indicate when something happened (year, day or month), how long ago it happened or how old the person is. It is best not to encourage prophetic people to try to figure out how to interpret a word of knowledge. (Remember my "green garden hose" misinterpretation?) It is best just to speak whatever the revelation is without an interpretation. Allow the Holy Spirit to be the interpreter.

Sometimes words of knowledge identify not the problem but the person with the problem. Sometimes you get an age, a name or the kind of work they do. I was on a trip in Brazil and one of the team members got the word "Train." A man came and confessed he was a train operator, but he was having trouble with falling asleep on the job. He was terrified that he would cause an accident and people would get hurt. His sleep disorder was prayed for, and we heard that he was able to sleep normally at night and be refreshed and alert on the job.

Other times words may indicate what is wrong with the person or how an injury occurred. I took a team made up primarily of students from our Global School of Supernatural Ministry to Brazil with me. They had been taught only a few days prior to the trip how to recognize words of knowledge. Almost all of them were having their first experiences in giving words of knowledge, yet I was amazed at their accuracy. One student's word was "Mechanic/radiator." A scene involving a mechanic and radiator had come to him in a vision during church worship. I thought he had missed it, but in that service was a mechanic who had a radiator blow up on him that day. He had burned his hands and could not close them. He was instantly healed.

Another student on the team said she saw a "Cast." A woman came up who was in extreme pain from tendonitis. When she heard the word, she said, "That's my word!" Instantly healed of her pain, she went and cut off her cast.

Another student saw a left breast with cancer in it. This caused the young woman with the cancer to have such faith that when she went to touch her large tumor, which she could easily feel before, she discovered that all her pain had left and the tumor was gone!

As an important aside, I should mention what I teach in regard to words of knowledge about sensitive or private areas. If you are praying for someone of the opposite sex, never touch the person in a way that could be considered inappropriate. Even for places considered acceptable, I suggest taking it a step further to ensure that nothing detracts from the ministry taking place. For example, if you are a man praying for a woman with shoulder pain, ask her permission to touch her even in what would be considered an appropriate place. Why? If a man has ever abused her, she could be very uncomfortable with being touched, period. Asking permission removes the forced contact and respects her boundaries. If she is uncomfortable with a touch on the shoulder, you can ask, "May I lightly touch your forehead, or would you prefer that I pray without touching you?" If the prayer involves an inappropriate area, as in the case of the breast tumor, you should ask the woman to lay her own hands on the area. If she is married, another possibility is to have her husband then lay his hands on her hands, and then you can lay your hands on the husband's.

Keep in mind that often people may be more comfortable with where you touch them than *you* are. You never should allow a person to take you beyond your own boundaries of appropriateness. You want to focus on the prayer for healing without subjecting yourself or the other person to moral temptation or conflict. As an example, one time in Brazil a man told me he suffered from terrible hemorrhoids. I laid my hands on the belt area of his back in what was an appropriate place to touch him and began to pray. To my surprise, he grabbed my hand, moved it to his hemorrhoids and said, "Not there, here!" He was trying to hold my hand in place while I was trying to move it, which embarrassed me. A wise response in such a situation would be to pray a short prayer of command and then move to the front and interview the person about how he or she is doing.

## The Power of Words of Knowledge

It would be unfair to end this chapter's teaching without giving some indication of the power of words of knowledge on people's lives. The words do create faith and bring healing, but words also have the power to change lives.

Tom Jones, the executive director of Global Awakening, pastored a large Pentecostal church prior to coming on staff with me. The first time I went to Tom's church, God gave my small team of four many words of knowledge. What was unusual was the number of words to which one woman responded. She stood up for eleven words of knowledge and was healed of every condition the words indicated. She had been in a terrible car accident that had caused all her physical problems.

As she continued to stand up for one word after another, I remember telling this woman, "God must really love you."

That night, an angel came into her room and said, "They missed one—the detached retina. I have come to heal it."

As a result of her healing experience, she and her husband, who were up until then nominal Christians, became one of the most on-fire couples in Tom's church. Their lives changed, and they later became full-time missionaries in Brazil. To this day, they continue as sold-out Christians, and I recently hired the husband, who joined the Global Awakening staff as director of our International Ministry Trip department.

Back when my wife and I moved to St. Louis to start a new church, which I told you about in chapter 1, we did not know anyone and there was no group waiting to join us. It was difficult, and it took us about two years to gather enough core people to have our first public service. We had been meeting in the basement of a home for those two years, and we had called twenty thousand people to tell them we were starting a new church for people who did not fit into "normal" church. About ninety new visitors came on that first Sunday, and about fifteen of them became part of our church. Those fifteen all were people who had received words of knowledge about their illness or words of knowledge about their lives in that first Sunday morning meeting.

I gave many words of knowledge that first meeting, probably over twenty-five, whereas I would usually receive half a dozen or fewer. But I had been praying about the service for weeks, and it was not a traditional service. For the fifteen who received those words of knowledge and stayed with us long-term, the reality of the experience was stronger than their sense of feeling uncomfortable with the unusual manner of our service. It is interesting that if you are reaching out to people who have never been in church before, the type of service we had that day is actually less uncomfortable than "normal," traditional church!

Many of those fifteen people also had special gifts we needed in the church. Our greatest need was for a dynamic worship leader. One of the words of knowledge was for a young woman suffering from hemorrhoids due to pregnancy. This word had come to me several days prior to the Sunday service. The young woman was there, pregnant, suffering and in pain.

When I gave the word, I said, "I don't want to embarrass anyone, so if you have this problem, later in the service go to one of our women on the ministry team and ask for prayer. You don't have to stand and identify yourself."

She received prayer and was immediately healed. She and her husband were so amazed that they started coming to the group in my home. They became one of the main couples with whom we would continue to build the church. Her husband was a tremendous musician and leader, and she had been a voice major with a college scholarship in voice. She had sung for the Pope in the Sistine Chapel. Extremely gifted in the arts, she wrote many powerful plays and musicals for our church.

My point is this: God was marking key leaders to help us build the church by revealing through words of knowledge their physical needs and healing them. Lives changed as a result.

I could say so much more about words of knowledge. In fact, I have written a whole booklet about them, *Words of Knowledge* (Global Awakening, 2001). In this chapter, though, I have tried to include the most important aspects of that teaching for you. I want to conclude by telling you how I first learned about words of knowledge, how I gave my first word of knowledge and what happened as a result of stepping out in faith.

I learned about words of knowledge through a telephone conversation with Lance Pittluck, a Vineyard leader while I was still a Baptist pastor. He told me that by interviewing numerous people who moved in this gift, they had discovered five ways the words came. He explained them to me this way:

1. You can feel them. The pain is not your pain; it is sympathetic.
2. You can think them. The thoughts come when you are *not* trying to think of a word of knowledge—they just come. They may be split-second or repetitive.
3. You can see them. This can be similar to a daydream, or it can be an open vision where you do not see anything else, but see something like a large-screen TV open in front of you.
4. You can read them. You actually see words on or over a person, or the words look like newspaper headlines or the captions at the bottom of a TV program.
5. You can say them. This is like tongues in that you do not think of what is said—it just comes out. It often will surprise you and open up the people you are ministering to as if the words spoken were a key to unlock the issues behind their sickness.

In only a very few minutes, this Vineyard leader had given me priceless information. Within a few days of our conversation, I began having words of knowledge, and I soon gave my first one. I was not sure it was God, so I gave it with fear and trembling. I received it while with a group of people in my Baptist church. While we were praying for someone who was sick at home, I felt a quick, jabbing pain in my left eye. I asked myself, *Is this a word of knowledge or is it just my pain?* And I thought, *If I try to give this word of knowledge and I am wrong, it will cost me the respect of the church's leaders.*

With great difficulty, it had taken me almost seven years to earn their respect. They had had difficulty believing an educated minister could be anointed by the Holy Spirit. Seminaries that taught cessationism and liberalism tended to put out the fire in the hearts of many graduates, as I mentioned in chapter 4. (In fact, the phrase sometimes used was that they had "graduated from the cemetery"!) I could lose the church leaders' respect much more quickly than I had gained it, but I thought, *If I give it and miss, I'll be humiliated, but I've been praying for humility. But if I don't give it, someone that could have been healed won't be. I think it's worth the risk.*

I stepped to the pulpit and said, "I think—that is, there might be someone here who—possibly—may have something wrong with their left eye." I was so worried I could be wrong.

Immediately a woman named Ruth stood and said, "That's my eye! I'm losing sight in it and now have only tunnel vision."

I was so excited that I had actually received a word of knowledge. Then it dawned on me that I had been told how to recognize words of knowledge, but the team from Vineyard had not come to teach us how to pray for the sick yet. I had gotten the cart in front of the horse! I did not know what to do or how to pray.

I was nervous that if I prayed and nothing happened, people would blame me and think I was not anointed. So I asked the whole church to come up so we could all pray for Ruth. My prayer was weak. It was long. I was afraid that when I stopped praying, I would find that nothing had happened. I kept right on praying, and God mercifully healed Ruth. But I realized then and there that I needed not only to know *how to get words* of knowledge; I needed to learn *how to pray* more effectively for healing. That will be the subject of the next chapter and its stories.

# 11

## THE RELATIONAL FIVE-STEP
## PRAYER MODEL

*Randy*

Todd White, a good friend of mine and an exceptional personal evangelist, has an amazing testimony. His family was falling apart from his years of drug addiction. While in Teen Challenge, he heard the voice of God tell him to leave and return home even though he had not completed the program. Despite the very high rate of recidivism among those who do not complete the entire program, Todd has remained drug free for many years. (This only worked because Todd discerned correctly that this was God's direction, not his own idea. If he had been wrong, he would most probably have fallen back into his addiction.)

Todd became a radical disciple of Jesus who took the Great Commission seriously: "Therefore go and make disciples of all nations, baptizing them in the name of the Father and of the

Son and of the Holy Spirit, and teaching them to obey everything I have commanded you" (Matthew 28:19–20). Jesus' instructions to the apostles point back to the commissioning of the Twelve and the seventy to heal the sick and deliver the demonized. Todd read in Mark 16:18 that whoever believes "will lay hands on the sick, and they will recover." He took this passage seriously and began to pray for the sick. Every day he prayed for ten or twelve people, but not one was healed.

Still, Todd did not doubt the Word of God. He did not start saying the Bible does not mean what it says. Instead, he questioned his own level of belief. He knew the problem was on his end, not God's. Todd continued to pray daily for people until he had prayed for about seven hundred people, with not one being healed. Then one day a man at work approached him, and Todd instantly knew what was wrong with him. This is a word of knowledge. Todd had never had one before and had not been taught about them. Yet he told the man what was wrong with his spine and leg, laid hands on him and prayed—and the man instantly was healed. In shock, the man tearfully told Todd he had had this condition for years. Since that day, Todd has been experiencing the truth of Mark 16:18, laying his hands on the sick and seeing them recover.

I was on an airplane with Todd one day. I watched him pray for every stewardess on the plane and every person seated around him. Several were healed. Then we decided to have lunch together before our connecting flights left. During lunch, Todd received and gave prophecies for the waitress, prayed for her and saw her physical condition healed. Todd prays for almost anything that moves. Whether or not he gets a word of knowledge, he will pray for people who tell him they have a physical problem. Not everyone is healed, but he sees a higher percentage of healings than most people I know.

## Co-laboring with Christ in Healing

The primary responsibility of discipleship is to hear the voice of the Spirit, then obey it. As the charismatically gifted people of the New Covenant, we are to continue the works of Jesus—especially in healing and deliverance—just as Todd does. Dr. Jon Ruthven's book I mentioned in chapter 3, *What Is Wrong With Protestant Theology?* (Word & Spirit Press, 2011), makes the accurate point that the New Testament's perspective on discipleship is very different from the usual understanding of discipleship that today's Protestants hold (and I believe Catholics hold, too). Paul said in 1 Corinthians 3:9, "For we are God's *co-workers*" (HCSB, emphasis added). However, we do not always see ourselves that way.

Let's think about this verse for a moment. The clearest revelation of God is His Son, Jesus. Paul said in Colossians 2:9, "For in Christ all the *fullness of the Deity lives in bodily form*" (emphasis added). The writer of Hebrews said, "The Son is the radiance of God's glory and the exact representation of his being," (Hebrews 1:3). Since the Son is the exact representation of God and the fullness of deity lived in Him, it seems proper to me to believe that what we saw Jesus do is the will of God. He revealed God's heart, manifested God's power and demonstrated God's love, especially through His ministry of healing and deliverance. And not just the apostles, but "we" are called to be God's co-workers, co-laboring with God.

Jesus said that whoever believed in Him would do what He had done and even greater works than these, because He was going back to His Father (see John 14:12). Jesus knew He would send the "Promise of the Father" once He ascended to the Father. The reason Jesus came was "to destroy the devil's work" (1 John 3:8). Acts 10:38 gives us insight into what that meant, at least in part: "God anointed Jesus of

Nazareth with the Holy Spirit and power," and Jesus then "went around doing good and healing all who were under the power of the devil, because God was with him." So we see that healing is one primary thing Jesus did in His ministry and one primary way He destroyed the devil's work.

Paul not only saw Jesus as the fullness of God, but he saw the Church as the fullness of Jesus: "And God placed all things under his feet and appointed him to be head over everything for the church, which is his body, the fullness of him who fills everything in every way" (Ephesians 1:22–23). These words come at the end of Paul's prayer for the Ephesians, which begins in Ephesians 18:

> I pray also that the eyes of your heart may be enlightened in order that you may know the hope to which he has called you, the riches of his glorious inheritance in the saints, and his incomparably great power for us who believe. That power is like the working of his mighty strength, which he exerted in Christ when he raised him from the dead and seated him at his right hand in the heavenly realms, far above all rule and authority, power and dominion, and every title that can be given, not only in the present age but also in the one to come.

If the Church is the fullness of Jesus, then it makes sense, does it not, that the disciples who make up the Church and who are co-workers with Christ should do the things He did? If you believe so, then what you are about to read will be helpful in getting started "doing the stuff."

### Getting Started Praying for Healing

Right in the middle of praying for Sister Ruth, whom I told about at the end of the last chapter, I realized I needed to

216

know more about how to pray for the sick. I had been told how to get words of knowledge, but I had not been told how to pray for the sick. I found the "Five-Step Prayer Model" I am about to share with you extremely helpful in getting started praying for the sick. When I learned it from John Wimber and his associates, I began to see many more people healed than before.

This Five-Step Prayer Model should not be looked at from a mechanical point of view. Rather, view it as a natural process of dialogue both with the person you are praying for and with God. It is a relational process, not a mechanical formula. And it is most appropriate to use it when praying for others in a pastoral context. Larger settings such as healing meetings or evangelistic outreaches require a different approach because this model would be difficult to employ in such a context. For example, in India where we might be praying for up to a hundred thousand people, trying to employ this model could result in the people we are praying for being crushed by the people behind them. In that setting it is not so much the gifts of healings that are being utilized, it is the authority for the Great Commission.

Note also that the Five-Step Prayer Model is not the only way to pray for the sick. I admit that there is not one specific "model" in the Bible. Jesus used many and varied ways of healing. Sometimes He touched people, sometimes He spoke their healing, sometimes He involved them in the process by asking for an act of obedience before the healing came. Sometimes He did bizarre things like spitting on His hand and then touching their tongues or making mud and putting it in their eyes.

Only one principle really pertains to Jesus' model for healing. His mother, Mary, reveals it. Before Jesus performed the miraculous turning of the water into wine, Mary said to His disciples, "Do whatever he tells you" (John 2:5). Follow that principle in praying for healing, and you will see amazing things. One of my most important points in this chapter is to help you learn how to hear what God tells you or how to see "what the Father is doing" right in front of you (John 5:19). This basic principle of discipleship is modeled after Jesus' relationship with the Father. Jesus perceived what the Father was doing. He heard or saw it and then obeyed. It is the same principle Mary illustrated when she told the bystanders to do whatever Jesus instructed them.

This is what makes Christian healing so different from Reiki and Therapeutic Touch. We are not learning how to channel impersonal power. That would be sorcery. We are not learning how to use impersonal power to balance someone's energy. We are not independent agents. Instead, we are in a dependent relationship with God. We are not making Him our servant— quite the opposite. We are yielding our lives to become His servants. As we come into relationship with Jesus and the Father through the Holy Spirit, we enter into a war against the works of the devil. Sickness, disease, pain, demonization and damnation are destroyed. We work *with* the Holy Spirit. That is the difference between a theistic religion like Christianity and pantheistic religions like Buddhism, Hinduism and New Age.

## Holy Spirit Etiquette

With this understanding of co-laboring with God and our dependence on God's power and energy, we need to think about what I call Holy Spirit etiquette. For example, when we ask God to do something and He does it, naturally we are both excited and thankful. We should immediately thank Him for honoring us with His presence and doing what He did. This is true whether our prayers are petitions or commands. (By petitions I mean prayers addressed to God; by commands I mean prayers addressed to a body part, a demon or an afflicting spirit.)

Since I cannot fathom the inner workings of our Triune God, I often will say, "Thank You, Jesus! Thank You, Holy Spirit! Thank You, Father!" I pray this not in the sense of covering all the bases, but out of a relationship with our Triune God. To thank one and not the others does not fully appreciate the work of all three. If you think relationally and not just theologically, it makes sense to thank the fullness of God. Even Paul had a Trinitarian doxology, and we sing the doxology in many churches on Sunday. For the same reason we sing the doxology, I thank each one of the Trinity.

The Bible does not model just one always applicable, always correct way to pray for the sick. However, it does present some principles to apply, such as interviewing a person to find out what is wrong. Jesus did this. He also modeled receiving revelation from the Father regarding what to do. Jesus varied the ways He chose to minister and modeled a process of prayer selection based on the condition He was dealing with. He did not minister to the demonized in the same way He ministered to the sick or brokenhearted. He also modeled what to do when healing does not happen immediately—He re-interviewed the person and prayed again. He modeled what to do when an evil spirit does not come out when first commanded—He continued to tell it to come out. He modeled the importance of faith through His teachings and actions. And He modeled occasionally giving instructions for people to follow after they received prayer.

Paul also provided insight into how to pray and the relationship between prayer and faith. First, as we already saw, Paul revealed an important principle about us working with God when he said, "For we are God's co-workers" (1 Corinthians 3:9, HCSB). Second, Paul revealed the importance of the relationship between our faith and our words. In 2 Corinthians 1:20 he said, "For no matter how many promises God has made, they are 'Yes' in Christ. And so through him the 'Amen' is spoken by us to the glory of God." And in 2 Corinthians 4:13 he said, "It is written: 'I believed; therefore I have spoken.' With that same spirit of faith we also believe and therefore speak." Both of these passages indicate the close connection between our faith and our speaking.

## The Five-Step Prayer Model

Recently my personal assistant, Chad Cromer, was with me in the United lounge in Sao Paulo, Brazil. He noticed an older woman who appeared to be in pain. He used the Five-Step Prayer Model to pray for her, and she was healed of the back pain she had struggled with for fifty years. You will find this model useful, too, in many situations. Let's look at each of the steps more closely:

- Interview
- Diagnosis and Prayer Selection
- Prayer Ministry: Praying for Effect
- Stop and Re-interview
- Post-Prayer Suggestions

### Interview

Mark 9:21 contains an interview between Jesus and the father of a boy who needed healing. Jesus asked the boy's father, "How long has he been like this?" The father answered, "From childhood." Jesus was modeling how to ask for information pertinent to a person's condition and healing. During your interviews with people, you want to gather information that can make your ministry time with them more natural, loving and effective. I begin with questions such as, "What's your name?" "How can I pray for you?" "How long have you had this condition?" "Do you know the cause?" "Why do you think you have this problem?"

The purpose of an interview is to determine the root cause of someone's infirmity or sickness. Possible roots would be an afflicting spirit, sickness rooted in the soul (psychosomatic) or sickness from natural causes such as accident, injury, lifestyle or disease. During the interview, ask some probing questions: "Do you have a doctor's diagnosis?" "Did someone cause this condition?" "Have you forgiven him or her?" (Unforgiveness can be a major hindrance to healing.) "Did any significant or traumatic event happen to you within six months or a year of this condition starting?" These questions are helpful because before praying for physical healing, you may need to help the person with unforgiveness or with emotional wounds such as fear, shame and rejection.

During the interview, depend on the Holy Spirit. Quietly ask Him if He has anything to show you about the person's condition or its cause. *Listen!* He may give you a word of knowledge or a prophetic word that could cut to the primary cause of the illness, exposing its root.

Also during the interview, you should build faith and understanding in the person you are praying for. I usually say the following to people:

About 50 percent of people who are healed feel something when I pray—heat, electricity, tingling, coolness, pain going away or getting worse. If pain gets worse, don't be discouraged. That means it's caused by an afflicting spirit, and the increased pain tips us off. But if that's the case, don't worry— if you spot them, you've got them!

The other 50 percent of people who are healed don't feel anything, they just get better. My faith isn't in what you feel.

But if you do feel something, be sure to tell me, because this can help me know how to better pray for you.

Also, about 15 percent of people are not healed when I pray, but are healed within a few days afterward. Again, my faith isn't in what you feel, but in the Word of God. But it's important for you to tell me what you're feeling; don't wait for me to stop and ask. Tell me immediately when you begin to feel anything. Tell me if whatever you feel increases, decreases, moves, anything. Do you understand?

In the interview step, you gather information that helps you determine the cause of someone's problem so you can best minister healing. You also need to share with that person what he or she can do to work with you for a better outcome. Ask the person not to pray, but instead, to close his/her eyes and focus on his/her body. It is a time for that person just to receive. I also ask the person not to make declarations or confessions while I am ministering, but to dial down and pay attention to his/her body. I mention again before I pray that if the pain increases, decreases, changes or moves, to tell me immediately. I also make sure that if the person appears weak, or if I think for some reason he or she might receive ministry better while seated, I get a couple chairs so we can sit down.

### Diagnosis and Prayer Selection

Based on the information you gathered in the interview and on any revelation God has given, the next step in this prayer model is to make a diagnosis about the root cause of a person's problem. In light of the root cause, you pray differently for different things, as Jesus did. Your prayer selection is related to the cause.

Jesus did not say pray for the sick, He said to *heal* the sick. When you read the gospels' stories about healings, notice that Jesus and His disciples never prayed petitionary prayers for healing. Instead, they commanded in prayer every time. Their prayer commands were not directed toward God, but toward people's conditions. Here are some examples of prayers of command I have used:

> *In the name of Jesus, I command the inflammation in Joe's knee to be healed, and all swelling and pain to leave. Swelling, pain, leave now!*

> *I command this high blood pressure to come down to normal pressure!*

> *I command this tumor to shrink! Wither! Disappear! I curse it!*

> *I command the DNA to be rewritten and to give a new message to the body, the message God designed and planned [used when praying for a genetic disorder]. I command the DNA to change and be normal.*

You should use commands most of the time, but especially in these instances:

- When breaking a curse or vow
- When casting out an afflicting spirit or other evil spirit
- When using petition prayers and healing progress has stopped
- When being led by the Spirit to use command prayers
- When ministering in evangelistic crusades that involve healing (command prayers of authority are particularly appropriate in these situations)

It is important to understand the connection between revelation and the authoritative use of command prayers. For example, if I said, "John Doe, I want to give you fifty dollars to help you buy gas," and John responded, "Randy, will you give me gas money?" that would be an inappropriate response on John's part. Instead of receiving the fifty dollars, thanking me and buying gas, he is asking me to give him what I *already* said I would. This makes it seem as if John does not believe me or my word. In like manner, I once was praying for people using words of knowledge to build faith. I received a clear, strong word of knowledge for one person and prayed, "God, I ask You to . . ." It suddenly hit me how inappropriate my prayer was, so I stopped. I said, "God, I'm sorry I just asked You to do what You just told me You wanted done." Then I commanded the condition to be healed in the authority of Jesus' name—and it was.

An example of petitionary prayer would be, "Father, in Jesus' name I ask You to heal the inflammation in Joe's knee and take out the swelling and pain." I do not think this is as powerful as a prayer of command in which you say, "In the name of Jesus, I command the inflammation in Joe's knee to be healed, and all swelling and pain to leave!"

Petitionary prayer belongs more in a worship context rather than in the context of evangelistic crusades where you are praying for healing. Petitionary prayers are more directed toward God and are relational, indicating our sense of dependence on Him. Commanding prayers are directed toward the problem, not toward God. They indicate our understanding of our God-given authority for healing and our understanding of what He wants to do, both generally speaking and in the particular situation. The specific sense of what God wants to do in a particular situation is gained through the gifts of the Holy Spirit, especially words of knowledge.

There is a place for mixing these two forms of prayer, especially when praying for other believers in church rather than for unbelievers in larger meetings. For example, I will often pray petitionary prayers like, "Come and help me, Holy Spirit. Show me what's wrong here, and teach me how to pray in this circumstance." I often pray these petitionary prayers softly. They are addressed to God, not to the person I am praying for. When I feel I am in spiritual warfare, I will quiet my spirit and speak to God alone, "Father, help me. Send Your angels to strengthen me and fight on my behalf." I ask God for revelation, for understanding and for provision in the natural, but I do not ask God to heal. He has delegated authority for that to His disciples.

Jesus often modeled the appropriateness of petitionary prayer. His parables of the unjust judge and the widow, and the friend knocking at the door at midnight, are two examples (see Luke 18; Luke 11:5–13). Other examples are His teaching in John 14 where He emphasized asking the Father in His name, and His own high priestly prayer of John 17, and also in the Garden of Gethsemane. However, neither Jesus, His disciples, nor others in the New Testament prayed petitionary prayers for healing.

The two types of prayer I am talking about might work together like this: You might petition God until faith is present and the purpose of God is determined, and then command a condition to be healed. This indicates both dependence on God and authority in Him. Or to put it another way, combining these types of prayer shows that there is a time to wait on God, and then a time as His co-workers to speak on His behalf. Elijah gave us an example of how to move from petitions to commands when he first petitioned God and then commanded the weather according to his words. The prayer of the righteous is powerful and effective! (See James 5:13–18.)

Based on the interview step, you determine whether to command an afflicting spirit to leave, command a tumor to disappear, command a leg to grow out if it is shorter or command pain to leave whatever area. If you perceive that a condition is psychosomatic in nature, though, you would not pray commands at first. To begin with, you would lead the person to forgive anyone toward whom he or she harbors unforgiveness. Unforgiveness is our inappropriate response to offenses that occur in interpersonal relationships, and it can be a blockage spiritually, so ask people to specifically forgive whatever another person did to hurt them. Then you can command their condition to leave.

Dealing with the psychosomatic roots of illness is a significant aspect of ministering healing. Over seventy years ago, the English Methodist pastor Dr. Leslie Weatherhead understood the theory that many medical conditions had psychosomatic roots. He predicted that what was then only theory would one day be proven by medical science, and he was correct. The field of medical study related to this area is now called psychoneuroimmunology. I have read in medical sources that 80 percent or more of illnesses are psychosomatic. In his book on rheumatoid arthritis, one medical doctor stated that if he could get people to forgive specifically—not just generally, but very specifically—the people who had hurt them, in many cases it would stop the progression of their disease. However, if they only forgave generally, their disease either did not change or continued to worsen.

Afflicting spirits cause some illnesses and pains. If a person tells you his or her pain worsens when prayed for, or if you experience this yourself when you begin to pray for someone, do not be discouraged. This is almost always an indication that the cause of the illness is an afflicting or demonic spirit. If the pain leaves one spot but goes to another part of the body, that also indicates the presence of an afflicting spirit.

In summary, in order for long-term healing to take place, the root cause of illness must be dealt with. The most common roots are these:

- Psychosomatic issues—the main root of many illnesses
- Natural causes—accidental injuries or carcinogens causing cancer
- Genetic causes—generational curses
- Afflicting spirits
- Lifestyle issues—neglecting scriptural teaching regarding rest, diet, exercise, stress

These areas weaken our immune system. They also require different prayer approaches. If a medical condition's root is psychosomatic, walking the person through forgiveness will almost always be part of your ministry. Once you get that behind the person, then you can command the condition to leave and command the body to come in line with heaven's pattern and God's will, according to Matthew 6:10, "Thy Kingdom come, Thy will be done in earth, as it is in heaven" (KJV).

If an afflicting spirit is causing a condition, command the spirit to leave in the name of Jesus. You may have to repeat this command many times. If natural reasons are causing a medical condition, again command the problem to be gone and command whatever needs to be repaired or recreated to happen. For example, "I command a new eardrum to be formed in Jesus' name" might be a prayer for healing deafness or impaired hearing. Or for genetic causes, "I command the DNA to be rewritten, come in line with heaven's pattern and be normal. I command the chromosomes to change, to be perfect in Jesus' name."

In December 2010, I was ministering in Brazil. I was praying for two people at once in a large church. I had begun praying with one, when the other came in who looked like he was in terrible pain. I kept my right hand on the first person and interviewed the second. (So many people needed prayer that it overwhelmed my prayer team, so I told them God gave us two hands so we could pray for two people at once.) During my interview with the second man, he was in such pain he could barely stand. He used a cane because he had had an accident five years ago that resulted in six back surgeries. He had two rods, two bars and ten screws in his spine. I placed my hand on his spine, and knowing his condition was accidental, I continued to pray for the first person and directed only a few brief commands toward this second person. He surprised me when he fell to the floor. He dropped to his knees, placed his forehead on the floor and stooped over for some time. I left my hand on his back and continued to pray for the first person. Then he stood up and said with great joy, "All my pain is gone!"

When I realized what had happened, I stopped praying for the first person to interview the second. He had been healed. I had spoken few words, but those were commands. I knew that sometimes healing virtue flows into people's bodies, and I often tell them that I am praying for them as long as my hand is on them. Even when I am not talking, I am praying—prayer is not only talking to God, but also listening for God and commanding on His behalf. I was surprised by how fast the man had been healed.

### Prayer Ministry: Praying for Effect

After the interview, diagnosis and prayer selection, the third step in the Five-Step Prayer Model is to begin ministering to the person by praying for effect. You are not praying to comfort the person, and you are not addressing your prayer for his or her ears as a form of psychological encouragement.

Rather, you are praying for effect. You also are aware that people feel things sometimes, even when you may not. This is vitally important when multiple things are wrong with a person and you may not have any leading from God on where to start.

In that case, I often begin with the simple petition, "Come, Holy Spirit, and show us what You're doing." By this I mean either by revelatory gifts such as a word of knowledge, word of wisdom or prophecy, or by the person feeling the presence of the Holy Spirit. I also pray, "Come, Holy Spirit, and touch John Doe. Show us where to start praying for healing. Come and touch his body." Then I wait.

I keep my eyes open most of the time so I can see when the Spirit first begins to touch people. They may tremble or perspire, their skin may blotch, tears may fill their eyes or run down their cheeks. Or while I am praying, I may notice that something I say causes a troubled look or furrowed brow. But often, people will begin to feel something long before you can detect it by watching. That is why it is so important for them to tell you the moment they feel anything.

Remember, no one in the Bible ever prayed for healing with the words, "If it be Your will." Neither do we see modeled anywhere in the New Testament someone praying for healing using petitionary prayers rather than commands. We should not beg God for healings, remind Him of the person's merit (as if that would move Him more than what his own Son did to merit the person's healing), or pray long, flowing prayers void of coming to the point of command. Remember, you are not commanding God to do what you say. You are commanding the body to respond because you are an ambassador—a representative of God's Kingdom with authority and power to heal the sick and cast out evil spirits. If after a while, the way you are praying is ineffective, change it. Perhaps your diagnosis of the root cause was wrong and the prayer needed is different due to a different root.

One night in Brazil, a woman on our team prayed for a blind man for over five hours. He had been blind since he was a small boy, and during the interview she discovered a natural cause. He had spilled acid in his eyes while young. Instead of big, brown Hispanic eyes, he now had nothing but white scar tissue where the cornea and pupil should have been. He never felt anything during her prayer—no heat, electricity, tingling or gradual improvement. Nothing. However, the woman sensed a strong urging from God to continue praying. She obeyed and prayed until we had to leave, some five hours later.

The woman went back the next day to the United States. I went to another city in Brazil and was joined by another team from the States. There, I received a telephone call from the church of thirty thousand members where the woman had prayed for the blind man. It was Pastor Aluisio Antonio Silva of the Videira Church in Goiania, Brazil.

Pastor Aluisio told me with great excitement, "It is the greatest miracle in the history of our city! A woman on your team prayed for this blind man for five hours, but he was no better. For the next two days nothing happened, but when he woke up on the third morning, he had new eyes and perfect vision. He is right now down at the hospital. This is the third trip. They keep asking him the same question: 'Tell us again, how is it you can see?' This is a miracle!"

The woman who prayed had not felt anything, and neither had the blind man. But she was obedient to the impressions she was having. She was persistent. Again, this brings us to the bottom line in ministering healing—the words of Mary about Jesus when she told the bystanders, "Do whatever He tells you." Today, Jesus as the head of His Church speaks to us through the Holy Spirit. It is the Holy Spirit who gives the gift of faith for miracles, who gives the revelation of the will of the Father and Son through words of knowledge and other gifts of the Spirit, who gives us the power to work the miracles and the healings.

Also remember that praying for healing is not the time to give advice or preach to the person. It is the time to expect the healing to happen and to speak—declare—command—what needs to happen. If a specific prayer brings improvement, keep using it in that situation. Some people want to accept their healing after your first prayer, even when they are getting better. I always tell them that we need to continue praying. We want the full manifestation of the healing now. As long as God is touching them, we should continue working with Him.

I mentioned what I call "Holy Spirit Etiquette" earlier, which I teach people to develop. Nowhere is this more appropriate than in the actual ministry time. When whatever we ask or command in Jesus' name begins to happen, we need to give thanks. Since all Three in One are involved in how healing is made possible, I say, "Thank You, Holy Spirit. Thank You, Jesus. Thank You, Father." Thanksgiving and praise are so important in the healing process. In my opinion, when the Triune God who created and sustains our universe gets involved in our local situation, we should naturally respond with joy and excitement. And when I am transparent about *my* excitement, it builds faith in the person being ministered to. Therefore, I express my thanksgiving, praise and excitement publicly—loudly enough for the person to hear me.

I also talked earlier about praying both prayers of petition and command, or combinations of the two. Pray "in the name of Jesus." But remember, our faith is not in this Five-Step Prayer Model, but in God. This model is only an attempt to help focus people on important principles related to healing and teach them to observe these principles while praying for the sick.

A couple stories illustrate what I am sharing. A few years ago I was in India, doing training in the daytime. The evenings were for open-air healing meetings with an evangelistic focus. Prior to the evangelistic sermon, much emphasis was given to healing through the word of knowledge. My team and I concluded the meetings by praying for the sick with the laying on of hands.

During one time of prayer, an older man was brought to me who could not walk. He had been carried to the meeting on the back of a friend. It actually hurt him to touch his feet to the ground. When I prayed for him, he mentioned through the translator that the pain was leaving his hips and increasing in his knees. I knew this was often a sign of an afflicting spirit. I switched from speaking to the pain and commanding parts of the body to be regenerated to commanding the spirit of affliction to leave his body. He told me the pain now was leaving his knees but was going into his feet. I continued to pray, commanding the spirit to leave his body in Jesus' name. He told me all the pain was gone in one leg, but was worse in the other foot. One last prayer of command resulted in all the pain leaving his body.

I told the man, "Your pain was caused by an evil spirit. I drove the spirit out by the authority of Jesus' name. Without Jesus in your life, you won't have any authority to keep the spirit out, but with Jesus in your life you have the authority to command the afflicting spirit to leave you when it tries to come back." Then I led him to Christ. The man who had been carried into the meeting on the back of his friend now walked home without any pain—and with Jesus in his heart.

We do not always understand what God is doing, as this next story shows. A friend of mine and his wife were powerfully touched by the Holy Spirit in a meeting Bill Johnson and I were doing in the United States. The experience radically changed their lives. I will call them Mike and Cindy. Their real names must be concealed for safety reasons. They live in an Islamic country and are engaged in evangelizing the Muslims of that country, which is illegal. In one village in the interior, where they had ministered for some time and had gained the respect of the local people, an event happened that confused them. They had befriended the most educated person in the village, who was responsible for turning in anyone who converted from Islam. This Islamic leader had seen many healings occur when Mike and Cindy prayed. One night their phone rang. It was the Islamic leader calling for Mike and Cindy. She said her mother was extremely ill, so Mike offered to visit the house. The leader was reticent. Mike told her, "This isn't about theology or whose religion is correct—this is about your mother's life."

The leader agreed that they could come over. When they arrived, several other members of the family were present. Mike thought, *Lord, what a great time for You to reveal Yourself to this Muslim family.* Mike and Cindy entered, laid hands on the mother and prayed in Jesus' name, but nothing happened. They left the village the next day to drive about eight hours to a large city. On the way, their cell phone rang.

"Mike, after you left, my mother's condition took a turn for the worse. We had to take her to the city, to the hospital. My family is angry with me for allowing atheists to pray for her." (Muslims consider Christians either atheists or polytheists.)

Mike did not understand why the mother had not been healed. He was confused because instead of bringing this family to Christ, the incident appeared to harden them to the

Gospel. Then the Holy Spirit told him to drive to the city, go into the hospital, and pray again for this mother. He obeyed. This time the whole extended family was present, over forty people in the room and in the hallway. The mother was now in critical condition and was not expected to live. Mike laid his hands on her and prayed again in Jesus' name. He still does not know why the family allowed him to do so. This time God healed her almost instantly!

When Mike was on his way home, the Holy Spirit told him that by not healing her the first time, more of her family saw the power of God in Jesus' name the second time. And in the extended family at the hospital, more strategic people were present who needed to see the miracle.

### Stop and Re-Interview

Mark 8:22–25 gives us the only example in the Bible in which Jesus did not heal someone instantly and completely the first time He ministered to the person:

> They came to Bethsaida, and some people brought a blind man and begged Jesus to touch him. He took the blind man by the hand and led him outside the village. When he had spit on the man's eyes and put his hands on him, Jesus asked, "Do you see anything?"
>
> He looked up and said, "I see people; they look like trees walking around."
>
> Once more Jesus put his hands on the man's eyes. Then his eyes were opened, his sight was restored, and he saw everything clearly.

I thank God this instance is recorded in the Bible, for it shows how Jesus ministered when healing did not happen the first time. What did He do? Assume healing must not be the Father's will? No. Did He figure that in the sovereignty of God the man would not be healed? No. After interviewing the man and finding out the healing was partial and incomplete, Jesus simply ministered again. This time the healing was complete.

This passage shows us some things. First, it is good to stop and re-interview after our initial time of ministry. Second, if the healing is only partial, we should continue ministering. I have seen many people pray for someone's healing and never ask if the person is better. Perhaps they are afraid that the person might not be healed, and then they would not know what to do next. Some people believe it would be wrong to pray a second time because it would show a lack of faith the first time. But we see Jesus doing this very thing—ministering a second time when the first time did not bring the desired result.

We should continually listen to the Holy Spirit and stop to re-interview a person as frequently as necessary to determine what is happening. Especially if nothing seems to be happening, you may want to re-interview the person. I periodically ask, "What is going on?" This is a way of "seeing" what the Father is doing.

Other questions you might want to ask are "Would you try again to remember any significant event?" "Have any other members of your family ever had this condition?" "Do you have a strong fear of anything?" "Has anyone ever pronounced a curse over you or your family?" "Do you know of anyone who is angry with you?" "Have you ever participated in any kind of satanic or other occult activity?" "Has anyone in your family been a member of the Freemasons?" (A very syncretistic group involving a vow to do harm to the body if its secrets are divulged. In the eyes of many who do deliverance, it is unwise to join it.) "Have you had other accidents?" (He or she may be accident prone, which can have a root in an inner vow, a bitter root judgment or be caused by an afflicting spirit. For more details, see John and Paula Sandford's *The Transformation of the Inner Man* [Victory House, 1982].)

How do you know when it is time to stop praying? You can stop when the person is healed, when he or she wants you to stop, when the Holy Spirit tells you to stop or when you are gaining no ground and receive no other way to pray. You realize at that point that you have no expectancy left with which to pray. It does not mean nothing has happened in response to your prayer—think of Mike and Cindy's story. You just do not yet know what God is doing.

An event from my ministry in Goiania, Brazil, illustrates the re-interview step. I was praying for a blind woman and asked her about any trauma, but she told me there had been none. The only thing bad that had happened was her father's death, but that had been several years ago. I prayed, commanding her eyes to see, for all parts of the eyes that were not working to work, for any part of the eye that had degenerated to regenerate. Nothing was happening. I stopped and re-interviewed her. I did not think her condition had psychosomatic roots. There was also no indication of experiencing more pain anywhere, so I did not think it was an afflicting spirit. No one was mad at her or her family, so I did not think it was a curse. I asked her more questions, but no clues were forthcoming. Then I had an impression, and the Holy Spirit was the source of my next question: "How soon did the blindness begin after your father's death?"

She told me, "It was instant."

I asked her, "Were you with your father when he died?"

She responded, "Yes."

I asked, "Were you touching him when he died?"

Again, she responded, "Yes."

Instantly, the Holy Spirit gave me a gift of faith. I was 100 percent confident this was not blindness with a natural or psychosomatic cause, but was in fact caused by an afflicting spirit that had something to do with her father's death. I did not even understand why I knew the cause—I just knew. The gift of faith can be hard to understand because it is not based on a rational conclusion or thought process. It comes as a gift.

I told her, "I'm going to pray for you one more time. This time when I finish, you'll be able to see." (I do not encourage anyone to make such statements apart from experiencing the gift of faith.) I prayed, and she could see. Had I not gone back and re-interviewed the woman, I might not have discovered the root cause of her blindness. This happened in Brazil on a night in which five other blind people were healed. Her healing was unusual, though, in that it was almost immediate. It is much more common for eyesight to be restored gradually over time, sometimes up to half an hour or more.

If you think you are operating in the gift of faith, it does not make any difference how much faith the other person has. If it is truly a gift of faith, whatever you command happens. If nothing happens, you were not really the recipient of a gift of faith.

On a final note about ministering effectively in prayer, we must be very careful not to align ourselves with or cooperate with the workings of the devil rather than the ministry of the Holy Spirit. When Jesus talks about the Holy Spirit in John 16:7, He refers to "the Counselor," which is an English translation of the Greek word *Paraclete*. The Amplified Bible notes that *Paraclete* could also be translated Comforter, Helper, Advocate, Intercessor, Strengthener and Standby. This Greek word literally means "the one who is called to stand by you and help you in your need." So if we need comfort, He is the Comforter, if help, He is the Helper . . .

*Satan*, on the other hand, means "the accuser of the brethren." We must be careful not to relate to people more like the accuser than like the Paraclete. The Holy Spirit comes to help us, not condemn us. Yet while in Brazil, I was shocked by one pastor's attitude toward someone in a wheelchair. This pastor had just prayed for the man and tried to pull him out of the wheelchair, but the man did not want to be pulled out. Perhaps he had had this experience too many times before. When the man's friends asked me to go pray for him, the pastor told me, "Don't pray for him; he doesn't have any faith." The pastor said this plenty loud enough for the man in the wheelchair to overhear. I ministered to the man anyway, over the pastor's objections. This pastor was moving more in the spirit of the Accuser than the spirit of the Comforter/Helper.

### Post-Prayer Suggestions

When you have finished the ministry time, it is beneficial to provide helpful follow-up instructions or exhortations. If you feel as though a person did not have faith, instead of condemning the person, you should help him or her grow in faith. If someone is not healed or is only partially healed, do *not* accuse the person of lack of faith or sin in his or her life. Rather, encourage the one receiving prayer with a Scripture or give him or her a good teaching series or book on healing to study. I often tell people that many who are not healed initially come back for more prayer later and *are* healed. I encourage people not to give up, but to continue receiving prayer for healing.

When people are healed, I encourage them with two recommendations. I tell them to thank God for whatever measure of healing they did receive and to ask for the rest if it was not complete. Also, I suggest that they tell family and friends about their healing.

Depending on the root cause of someone's condition, I may add other post-prayer suggestions. If a person's

238

condition was healed and its root cause was a lifestyle issue that resulted in poor health, then I encourage the person to make the necessary lifestyle changes to prevent the problem from returning.

If the root cause was an afflicting spirit, I mention that the symptoms probably will return. This does not mean the person has lost the healing. It means the afflicting spirit is trying to come back. The spirit may try multiple times to bring the sickness or pain back, but it must always be met with faith and commanded to leave. I tell the person, "If you respond to the first signs of symptoms in doubt and fear, thinking you have lost your healing, you will lose it. But if you respond with understanding, rebuking the spirit and commanding it to leave, you will keep your healing."

## In Jesus' Name

I want to end this whole chapter with an experience I had in the home of Pastors John and Carol Arnott during the early days of the outpouring of the Spirit in the mid-1990s in Toronto, in what became known by the press as the "Toronto Blessing," but what John liked to call the "Father's Blessing." I was in their guest bedroom, resting and meditating on what God was doing. I began to think about some of the healings that were beginning to happen. In the midst of my thoughts, I heard the strong internal impression from God, "I don't like your Five-Step Prayer Model."

I was aghast. I thought the model was biblical and modeled our dependence on God. I asked, "What don't You like about it, God?"

To which He responded, "It isn't what you're doing that I don't like—it's what you're not doing."

I asked, "What do you mean?"

Again His quick reply came, "There is no emphasis on praying in My Son's name."

That night when I returned to minister, if I prayed "In the name of Jesus" once, I prayed it at least a hundred times!

Again, let me state that this is not meant as a mechanical model for prayer. I do not even like the word *model*. I do not believe this is the only way to pray for healing, and at times this model cannot be used effectively, for example in large crusades. Yet it is a model built on seeing ministry as very relational and dependent on God—and it is all done "in Jesus' name."

My final word on this prayer model is that when we first heard about it in my Baptist church, the leader of the team that came to teach us said, "Don't go out and pray for a few people and come back and say, 'This doesn't work.' No! Go out and pray for two hundred people. If you do that, you will see enough people healed to hook you for life."

I hope the Five-Step Prayer Model I have presented gives you some clues about how to get started in co-laboring with Christ and obeying the Great Commission. But now it is time to stop reading about it and begin *doing* it. In the name of Jesus, go. Go do the stuff. Heal the sick and cast out demons. (Perhaps in a future book we will share how we minister to demonized people.) As you become God's co-worker and see people healed and set free, it will hook you for life.

---

*Father, I ask You to anoint those reading this book with an anointing for healing. I ask You to release words of knowledge to them and empower them for healing. May the power of Your Holy Spirit come upon them, and may it flow into them and then out of them into the people they will pray for in the future. In Jesus' name. Amen.*

# INDEX

241

# ABOUT THE AUTHORS

**Bill Johnson** is a fifth-generation pastor with a rich heritage in the Holy Spirit. Together, Bill and his wife, Beni, serve as the senior pastors of Bethel Church in Redding, California. They also serve a growing number of churches that have partnered for revival. This leadership network has crossed denominational lines, building relationships that enable church leaders to walk successfully in both purity and power.

The present move of God has brought Bill into a deeper understanding of the phrase "on earth as it is in heaven." Jesus lived out this principle by doing only what He saw His Father doing. Heaven was the model for Jesus' life and ministry—and Bill makes it his model, as well. Bill demonstrates how recognizing the Holy Spirit's presence and following His lead enables believers to do the works of Christ, destroying the works of the devil.

Bill and his church family regularly see healings in areas ranging from cancer to broken bones to learning disorders to emotional trauma. These works of God are not limited to revival meetings or church services. Bill teaches that believers need to take this anointing into schools, the workplace and their neighborhoods with similar results. We owe the world an encounter with God, he says, and a gospel without power is not the Gospel that Jesus preached. Bill believes that healing and deliverance must become the common expression of this Gospel of power once again.

Bill and Beni have three children and nine wonderful grandchildren. All three of their children are married and involved in full-time ministry with their spouses. To learn more about Bill Johnson, his ministry and his resource materials, visit www.ibethel.org and www.bjm.org.

### Other Books by Bill Johnson

- *The Center of the Universe*
- *Dreaming with God*
- *Face to Face with God*
- *Release the Power of Jesus*
- *Strengthen Yourself in the Lord*
- *The Supernatural Power of a Transformed Mind*
- *When Heaven Invades Earth*

**Randy Clark** is best known for helping spark the move of God now affectionately labeled "the Toronto Blessing." In the years since, his influence has grown as an international speaker. He continues, with great tenacity, to demonstrate the Lord's power to heal the sick.

Randy received his M.Div. from The Southern Baptist Theological Seminary, and he is presently working on his D.Min. from United Theological Seminary (Dayton, Ohio). His message is simple: "God wants to use you." He has written or helped compile seven books, including *There Is More*, sixteen booklets and four workbooks or training manuals.

The most important aspect of his calling to ministry is the way God uses him for impartation. John Wimber heard God speak audibly the first two times he met Randy, telling John that Randy would one day go around the world laying his hands on pastors and leaders for the impartation and activation of the gifts of the Holy Spirit. In January 1994, in the early days of the outpouring of the Spirit in Toronto, John called Randy and told him that what God had shown him about Randy was beginning now. It has continued ever since.

Randy has the unique ability to minister to many denominations and apostolic networks. These have included Roman Catholics, Messianic Jews, Methodists, many Pentecostal and charismatic congregations, and the largest Baptist churches in Argentina, Brazil and South Africa. He has also taken several thousand people with him on international ministry teams. His co-author, Bill Johnson, says the fastest way to increase in the supernatural is to accompany Randy on an international trip. Randy has traveled to over 36 countries and continues to travel extensively to see that God's mandate on his life is fulfilled.

Randy and his wife, DeAnne, reside in Mechanicsburg, Pennsylvania. They have four adult children, three of whom are married, and two grandchildren. For more information about Randy Clark, his ministry and his resource materials, visit www.globalawakening.com and RandyClarkMinistry.com.

**Other Books by Randy Clark**

- *Changed in a Moment*
- *Entertaining Angels*
- *God Can Use Little Ole Me*
- *Lighting Fires*
- *Power, Holiness and Evangelism*
- *There Is More*

### Booklets

- *Acts of Obedience: Relationship to Healing and Miracles*
- *Awed by His Grace/Out of the Bunkhouse*
- *Baptism in the Holy Spirit*
- *Biblical Basis for Healing*
- *Christ in You the Hope of Glory and Healing/Healing and the Glory*
- *Deliverance*
- *Evangelism Unleashed*
- *Falling Under the Power*
- *Healing and the Lord's Supper*
- *Healing Out of Intimacy with God*

- *The Healing Streams That Make up the Healing River*
- *Learning to Minister under the Anointing/Healing Ministry in Your Church*
- *Open Heaven*
- *Pressing In/Spend and Be Spent*
- *Thrill of Victory/Agony of Defeat*
- *Words of Knowledge*

### Ministry Materials—School of Healing and Impartation

- *Ministry Team Training Manual*
- *Deliverance, Disbelief and Deception*
- *Healing: Medical and Spiritual Perspectives*
- *Revival Phenomena and Healing*